THE FRENCH WINES

The French Wines

Georges Ray

Honorary Professor (Tunis, Rennes and Grignon)
Former Head of Technical Services at the International Institute of Agriculture, Rome

Translated from the French and revised, with additions, by Paul Capon

With 9 maps

WALKER AND COMPANY · NEW YORK

First published in France as Les Vins de France,
a title in the Que sais-je? series.

Published simultaneously in Canada
by George J. McLeod, Limited, Toronto.

Library of Congress Catalog Card Number: 65-15127

Printed in the United States of America
from type set in Austria

Contents

1. The Birth of French Wines; The Importance and Distribution of Vineyards **3**
2. From the Vine to the Glass **15**
3. A Survey of French Wines **23**
4. Eaux-de-Vie **73**
5. Allied Industries **83**
6. Wine and Food **91**
7. The Wine Cellar and Its Treasure **107**
Appendix I:The Composition of Wine **113**
Appendix II: Viticultural Evolution Since 1790 **115**
Appendix III: Cooperage **118**
Appendix IV: The best Vintages of Recent Years in Suggested Order of Merit **119**
Appendix V: Summary of French Wines **120**
Appendix VI: The Official 1855 Classification of the Great Growths of the Gironde **139**
Appendix VII: Outstanding Burgundies **144**
Appendix VIII: Capacity of Standard Bottles as Fixed by Decree **147**
Appendix IX: Conversion Table: Degrees of Alcohol and Degrees of Proof Spirit **148**
Index **149**

CHAPTER 1

The Birth of French Wines The Importance and Distribution of Vineyards

That France produces the greatest wine in the world can hardly be disputed, and that France produces the most wine of any country can be proved by statistics, so there at least I have two excuses for writing this short book concerning wine—not a weighty treatise, but a book for the pocket that can be taken anywhere and consulted effortlessly, humming a drinking song the while.

Although I hope I can add a little even to the expert's knowledge, my observations are intended primarily for the reader who wants to know the names and properties of the various wines, who perhaps wishes to start a cellar, and who certainly wants to overcome any apprehension he may feel when a waiter puts a wine list into his hands; and also, I write for the tourist in France who would like to visit some of the vineyards and wants to know which lie on his itinerary.

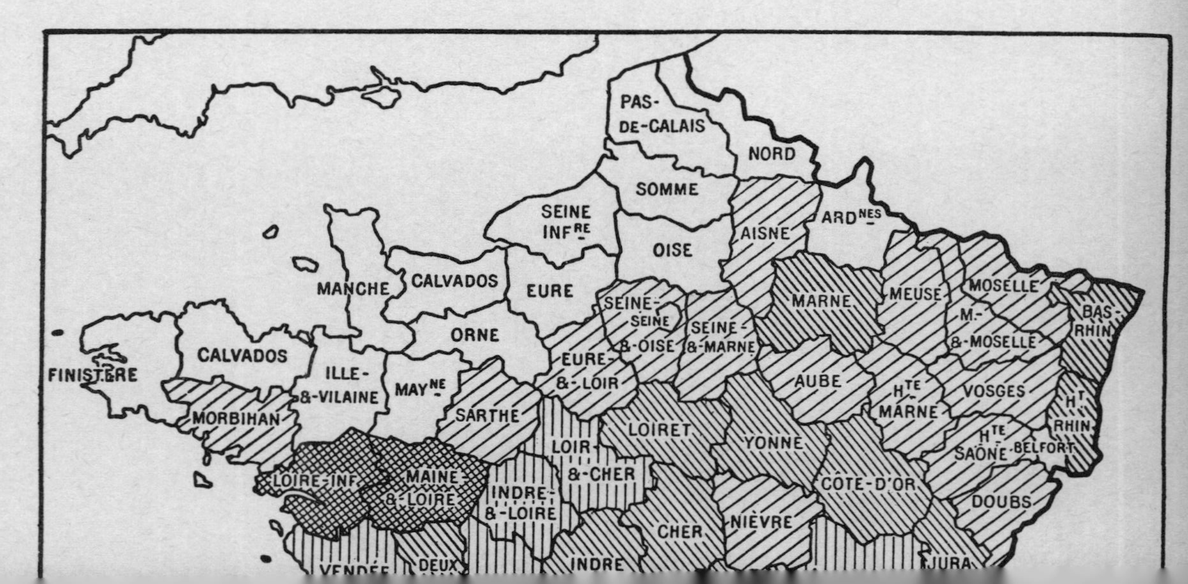
PAS-
DE-CALAIS
NORD
SOMME
SEINE
INF^RE
ARD^NES
AISNE
OISE
MANCHE
CALVADOS
EURE
SEINE-
SEINE
& OISE
SEINE-
& MARNE
MARNE
MEUSE
MOSELLE
M.-
& MOSELLE
BAS-
RHIN
ORNE
CALVADOS
FINISTÈRE
ILLE-
& VILAINE
MAY^NE
EURE-
& LOIR
AUBE
H^TE
MARNE
VOSGES
H^T
RHIN
MORBIHAN
SARTHE
LOIRET
YONNE
H^TE
SAÔNE
BELFORT
LOIR-
& CHER
LOIRE-INF.
MAINE
& LOIRE
INDRE-
& LOIRE
CÔTE-D'OR
DOUBS
CHER
NIÈVRE
VENDÉE
DEUX
INDRE
JURA

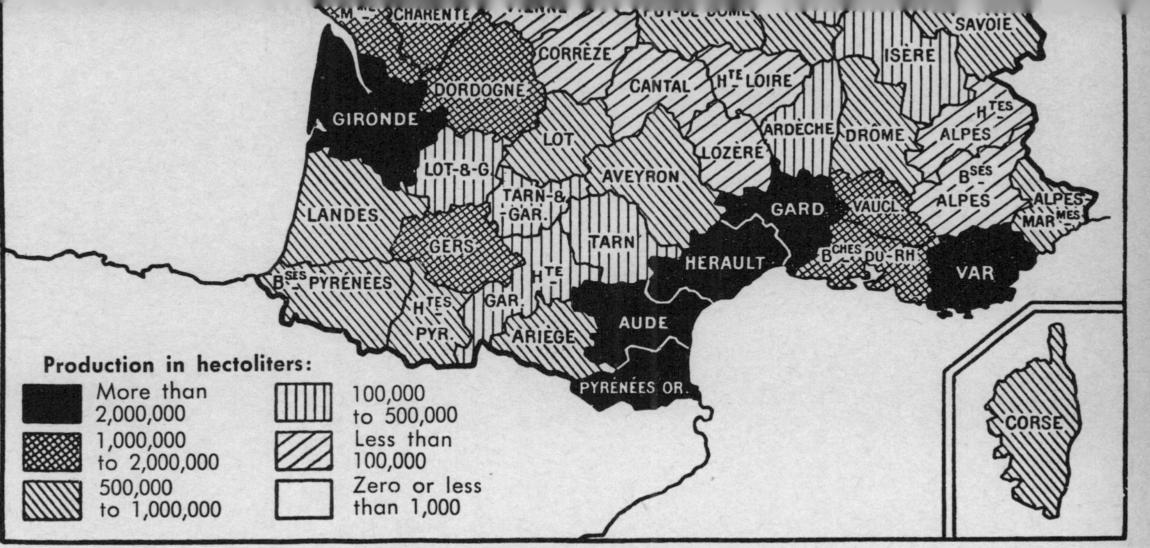

Fig. 1. Production of Wine (1930—1939)

So let us set out on a voyage of discovery, making a tour of the land, and omitting only a few districts in the north and the west that are innocent of vineyards and vines. We shall visit the vine-clad fields and hillsides, and we shall make our way into the depths of quiet cellars where, by candlelight, we shall raise our tasting glasses and compare the wine's ruby-red tones or golden tints with the flickering light shining through it; and, in the course of our pilgrimage, even the most indifferent eyes will be opened to that glory of France accumulated through the centuries—the grapevine's cultivation.

THE GRAPEVINE IN ANTIQUITY

Long before the dawn of history men living in what is now France cultivated the grapevine, and in the Champagne area the imprints of vine leaves have been found in strata dating from the Tertiary period. However, wine as we know it probably originated in Asia, and that great authority on wine, Camille Jullian, attributes the earliest knowledge of wine in France to the later Stone Age, "whose people cleared and tilled our land some four to five thousand years ago."

Mystical communion by means of bread and wine—a pagan tradition sensibly adopted by Christianity—is found as far back as we can go in the study of human rites, and if our distant ancestors had the ingenuity to make flour from barley, and bread from flour, how much easier was it for them to invent wine-making, when alcoholic fermentation would result of its own accord if grapes were crushed and the juice left to stand; and indeed neolithic remains prove that man early acquired a taste for fermented drinks.

There was a dark side to the picture, however: it was all too easy for wine-drinking primitive man, uncertain master of his desires, to cross that thin line separating jovial moderation from the excesses and violence of drunkenness. Then the guardians of moral sense—priests, druids and other ministers of the various deities—intervened without compunction, and punished temptation by ordering the uprooting of the vines. Traces of these early attempts at prohibition have been found in Rumania, in territory once occupied by the Dacians; and even in Gaul the same thing seems to have happened. In fact, there is evidence to suggest that men were forbidden to plant vines in Gaul before the Romans came, with the result that wine was imported from the country around Marseilles and from Italy, places where wine-growing flourished. Prices on this black market were exorbitant, one whole slave being paid for a single amphora of wine.*

Mankind learns but slowly from historical example, and we of the twentieth century can be ashamed of ourselves for once again attempting prohibition.

THE VINE IN HISTORY

An approximate date can be put to what Camille Jullian so rightly called the "birth" of our national drink. It was at Marseilles—then not part of France—that Greeks

*The Roman amphora contained five and a half gallons, and the Greek approximately eight and a half.

from Phocaea in Asia Minor founded a new colony about 600 B.C., and planted the first stocks. Five hundred years later the colonization of Gaul by the Romans removed the obstacles to wine-growing and the wine trade, and the "divine plant," as it was poetically called by another Julian—the Roman emperor of that name—began its conquest of the hinterland. This peaceful invasion, spreading from Marseilles, took two directions. Northward the vines' tendrils spread along both banks of the Rhône, and soon the slopes of the Côte-Rôtie acquired a fame that they have never lost. The Allobroges, whose tribal territory included the Rhône Valley, boasted that they grew the best wine in Gaul.

Westward from Marseilles the vine followed the Languedoc road and virtually smothered the countryside. Béziers, that ancient city perched comfortably on its hill, gave its name to all wine from that region; its wines rivaled those of Marseilles on the tables of Roman *bons vivants*. Although the flow of trade has changed its direction, Béziers still remains the controlling market for the wines of the Midi.

An incursion of less importance took the vine to Nice and the foothills of the Maritime Alps; the Greek- and Latin-speaking men who introduced it also introduced other benefits of ancient civilization. Other frontiers were quickly swept aside by the vine's advance, and, leaving the Rhône at Lyon, it ascended the Saône Valley, and gained the hillsides of the Côte d'Or, an area now so renowned for its wine. Thus Burgundy, until then a barley-growing district, became one of the grapevine's chosen provinces, to be numbered among those regions where the art of wine-making has approached perfection. A comparable divagation, and one that had similar results, took place westward from Languedoc, and the vine, following the Garonne's fertile banks, descended upon Bordeaux. In that region, on the sunny gravel banks (*les graves*) flanking the slopes above the river, there was soon not an estate to be found that did not have its vineyards.

Farther to the north the vine made its appearance in the Loire Valley and, less confidently, in that of the Marne, while the land drained by the Seine became an important wine-growing region, with Paris its center and the aforementioned Emperor Julian its leading customer. Vines were to be seen on the Sainte Geneviève hill, as well as all along the Seine's left bank, and although viticulture certainly appeared in other parts of what is now the capital, nowhere was it pursued more vigorously than at Vaugirard: that area, where nowadays we see dismal collections of soot-grimed buildings, was in earlier centuries the home of wines whose quality approached the most famous. This would be hard to believe were it not still possible to gaze upon Paris's last bed of hardy vine-plants on the top of La Butte, the last surviving vestige of vineyards that once produced Montmartre's *cru*. Right at the bottom of the hill the charmingly named Rue de la Goutte-d'or (drop-of-gold) reminds passers-by that as recently as 1842 this modest thoroughfare led into a once-famous vineyard.

The vine reached Alsace and the Rhine in the third century. By then France had suffered its first German invasion. France has known many others since, and the last is too recent to have escaped even our short memories. Each time the devastation has been enormous—the cellars have been robbed of their treasures, and the few vines that have escaped destruction have been, perforce, abandoned and neglected. For all that, when the barbarian hordes fall back, they can take no more with them than the soil that clings to their invading boots, and as soon as they have gone the ruined wine-growers return to their vines, and once again bravely take up mattocks and pruning knives. Little by little order is restored, and France lives on.

By the fourth century the vine had reached all the regions where it is still grown. By good fortune the Christian priests who replaced the Druids were by no means the enemies of wine that their predecessors had been. Indeed it can almost be said that wherever a monastery was founded, there vineyards were planted, and it is not surprising that one of the results of the Crusades was the appearance of new varieties of vine in France; the famous Pinot, from which all the great Burgundies are made, almost certainly came from the Near East at about that time.

Not all importations have been so successful, and the enterprising wine-grower who introduced some American vine-stocks into our country during the last century also introduced a voracious little insect called the phylloxera, which promptly devastated more than half of France's vineyards. Since then all French vines have been grafted onto American roots, which are more or less immune to the parasite.

DISTRIBUTION OF FRENCH VINEYARDS

The vine is a plant of the plains and the lower slopes, and it is exceptional for it to be grown above 1500 feet. It is virtually nonexistent in seven *départements* (Nord, Pas-de-Calais, Seine-Inférieure, Manche, Finistère, Côtes-du-Nord, Orne), and very little cultivated in a dozen others. As against this, there are some forty *départements* in which it has an important place.

Before we survey the several aspects of French viticulture, it would be advisable to adopt an over-all scheme, and although Dr. Jules Guyot's classification first saw the light of day three-quarters of a century ago, in the second edition of his *Etude des vignobles de France* (1876), it is still valid. Dr. Guyot divides France into eight wine-growing regions: (1) the Midi; (2) Bordeaux and the Southwest; (3) Charentes and the West; (4) the Southern Center; (5) Burgundy and the Northern Center; (6) the East; (7) Champagne and the Northeast; and (8) the Northwest.

Like all attempts at classification, this division is doubtless somewhat arbitrary. Nevertheless each of these regions is characterized well enough by the nature of its soil, the varieties of vine cultivated in it, the manner in which the vines are trained, and the method of wine-making used. In France it is the balanced combination of geographical position and human endeavor that produces an amazingly rich range of wines, and often we shall see tiny townships—so small that it is sometimes hard to find them on the map—emerge from the shadows solely because their wine has made them famous. Indeed in some places a field survey is needed rather than a map, for in the most celebrated wine-growing districts human ingenuity has created some vineyards of repute whose area must be measured by fractions of acres, and whose annual production gauged by numbers of bottles.

CHAPTER 2

From the Vine to the Glass

"THE WINE-GROWER CLIMBS TO HIS VINE"

As the song has it, "The winegrower climbs to his vine," and now let us go with him.

Under the first caresses of the springtime sun, the vine emerges from its winter torpor, and, from clean cuts inflicted on the shoots by the pruning blade, some drops of sap escape. These are lyrically known as "the grapevine's tears," but while the wine weeps the wine-grower rejoices at the prodigious cellular activity revealed by these drops. Already the buds are opening to allow the young leaves to shoot, and unless the vines are sprayed with a protective solution there is a danger of these leaves being blighted by frost some morning in the merry month of May.

Then the flower-clusters appear, which, though not remarkable for their color, fill the air with that subtle scent unsurpassed by any other flower, unless it be that of the lime tree. At this point the prospects of the still-distant harvest begin to take shape with the enlarging of the grapes, and these, which of course are at first hard and green, suddenly change color at the moment of ripening, the *veraison*. After some forty-five days the crop is thinned out and, with the sun's help, the bunches of grapes grow heavy, each grape becoming swollen with a juice whose acidity steadily diminishes as it increases its sugar content.

HARVEST TIME

Soon samples of the juice, tested with a densimeter, show that the sugar content has reached its maximum. This indicates that the fruit's living cells, each a miniature laboratory, have entered a period of relative inactivity. It is now that the order goes out to the gangs of vintagers to cut down the grapes, and this they do, taking care not to damage them. Then they transport the bunches to the pressing room, with all the respect due to the soil's most precious product.

Now we have to deal with the delicate process of fermentation, where carelessness and errors can cost us dear, and so accurate are the installations used for extracting the grape-juice that the strictest attention is necessary at every moment. That wine-making remains a difficult art is due to the exact knowledge needed of what happens during the fermenting of the must, and also during the period, often extremely long, when the wine is maturing; only with such knowledge can a product of good quality be confidently obtained. The time when this was an empirical matter has gone forever, and these days it is necessary to study chemistry and microbiology to control a process in which, as Pasteur and his disciples showed, the microbes, good ones or bad, are the masters.

THE RANGE OF WINES PRODUCED

Of course, here it is not possible to deal with the successive stages of wine-making in any detail, but what amazes the uninitiated on first entering a cellar is the wide range of wines all drawn from the same raw material—that is, grapes, which to look at them are almost identical. But the grapes that are best to eat are not the ones that make good wine.

The variety of vine best suited to the soil and the climate must be selected from an extremely long list—minutely described in the seven volumes of Viala and Vermorel's *Ampélographie*—and according to whether it produces a full-bodied wine needing time to mature, or an undistinguished wine, but one that gives a high yield. All the various factors relating to the vine's cultivation—its height, its degree of ramification, its training, pruning and thinning—affect the grapes in characteristic ways that will be reflected in the wine's quality, as will the mixing of grapes having different and often complementary merits. Finally, the seasons themselves, by influencing the number of hours of daylight and affecting the temperature curve, imprint their rhythm on the growth of the plants and on the grapes' ripening.

Sometimes this final stage is allowed to extend well into the autumn, with the object of increasing the sugar content of the juice and thus the alcoholic strength of the wine made from it. This is what takes place in regions—Sauternes, for instance—where the grapes are left on the vines until they wither a little under the action of that celebrated and noble mold *Botrytis cinerea*; and the winegrowers of the Jura spread the gathered grapes on straw beds so that the juice, enriched by natural reduction, can be used for making the famous straw wines. It is possible, moreover, to check the fermentation of the must by adding cognac or pure alcohol, and if the fermentation of the sugar takes place in sealed bottles the dissolved carbonic gas produces effervescence as soon as the cork is drawn—the essential characteristic of sparkling wine.

All those considerations, responsible for giving each wine its character, have to be carefully weighed before the most suitable method of wine-making is decided upon, and this applies both to ordinary wines that will appear on the customer's table in the year after the vintage, and to quality wines that are kept for several years in the cask and for anything up to twenty in the bottle, both for *pinard* and for the finest champagne.

Incidentally, where does that picturesque term *pinard* come from, which gained currency during World War I as a word for cheap wine, and which since 1943 has found a place in the French Academy's *Dictionnaire*? All that can be said is that for the Burgundians of the seventeenth century the virtues of the typical winegrower were personified by a certain Jean Pinard, and this is attested by the publication at Auxerre in 1607 of a book entitled *Discours joyeux en façon de sermon fait avec notable industrie par déffunct maistre Jean Pinard, lorsqu'il vivait trottier semi-prébendé en l'Eglise de Sainte-Etienne d'Auxerre, sur les climats et finages des vignes du dict lieu. Plus y est adjousté de nouveau le monologue du bon vigneron sortant de sa vigne et rentrant le soir en sa maison.* ("A cheerful discourse propounded with notable industry and in the form of a sermon by the defunct Master Jean Pinard, when he lived as a semi-prebendary in the precincts of the church at St. Etienne at Auxerre, dealing with the vineyards and vintages of that place; to which has been newly added the good vine-tender's soliloquys as he visited his vines and as he returned home in the evening").

Between the ordinary wines of the *pinard* type and the elaborately graded aristocracy of the vintage wines, there lies an imposing array of what we might call the middle-class wines, the tradesmen and peasants, full of solid virtues and accessible to a wide clientele. To mention all those deserving a mention and to make a viticultural tour, pausing at all the places where they are produced, would take far too long, so we must curb our ambitions and avoid losing ourselves in detail. Reflect that in a single vineyard the wine produced in a particular year will reveal differences even from one bottle to another, depending upon such factors as the care taken by the grower and the arrangement of the bins in the cellar where the maturing takes place!

"APPELLATION CONTRÔLÉE"

In the pages that follow, the words "appellation

contrôlée" will be used fairly frequently, and a note on what is implied may not be out of place.

Until the *Code du Vin* was formulated in 1936, many a bottle of wine was sold fraudulently, in that its label proclaimed it to be of much better origin than in fact it was. But all that has been changed, and if you read the words "appellation contrôlée" on a label, you can be quite certain that the wine comes from the place it purports to come from.

An exception to the rule is champagne, perhaps because it was the first wine to secure an official delimitation of its territory, and the traditional description "Vin de Champagne" is all the guarantee you need.

CHAPTER 3

A Survey of French Wines

Now we embark on a formidable task: to give, in a few pages, some idea of French wine production, describing the most famous wines of each region, those peerless jewels, either glowing in an elegant setting of more modest growths, or scattered here and there in areas noted for their high yield, yet whose products are not always devoid of merit. It would take a great deal of time and space to award each wine its just share of praise, and still we would be guilty of neglecting many. Moreover an inexhaustible supply of superlatives would be called for, since, rich as the French language is, it remains powerless to give an exact impression in black and white of the wine-taster's subtle sensations, more intangible than a symphony orchestra's sonorous tonalities.

WINES OF THE MIDI

Until the outbreak of war in 1939, wine-snobs hurled anathema indiscriminately upon all wines intended for ordinary consumption, but especially upon those from the most productive winegrowing regions such as the Midi, condescending to allow no more merit to such *pinard* than that it had brought comfort to the troops of the war before, that of 1914-18. Yet surely to consider one of the most important of French agricultural products as negligible is both unjust and stupid. Ordinary wine, well made and served straightforwardly (as is done in good houses) in the year after the harvest with no guarantee except its proof, constitutes a healthy drink, and one that forms a normal accompaniment to the family cuisine, the vintage wines being kept, and with good reason, for the splendor of special occasions.

For the most part, the Midi produces red wine from vines with a high yield, ones that give between fifty and a hundred hectoliters to the hectare, often more in the plains, and as much as two hundred hectoliters in irrigable areas such as the Camargue.* In the latter winegrowing is a full-fledged industrial undertaking, and the premises where the wine is made have developed into huge factories, frequently run on a cooperative basis. The wine is sold at prevailing prices according to its proof.

It was toward the middle of the eighteenth century that the grapevine started its conquest of the Midi's

*One hectoliter equals 26.418 gallons. One hectare equals 2.471 acres.

mountainous areas, ousting cereal crops and olives, and giving to a great part of the Mediterranean littoral the characteristics typical of a single-crop region. From the mountain slopes the vines spread to the plains drained by

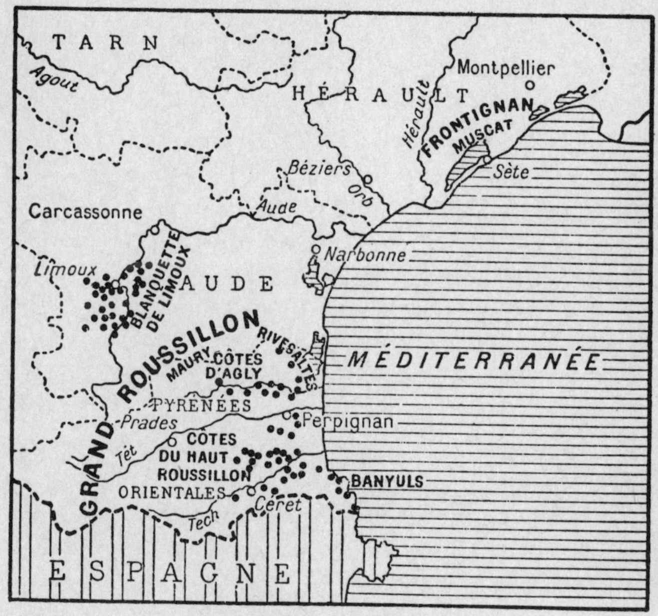

Fig. 2. Wines of the Southeast

the Rhône, the Vidourle, the Lez, the Hérault, the Orb, the Aude and the Têt, huge areas in which numerous varieties of vine flourish, such as the Aramon, the Carignan, the Petit Bouschat, the Oeillade and the Cinsaut, and many other plants whose untrained branches are allowed to spread freely over the ground.

It would be wrong to think that the areas with a high yield necessarily produce wines without character. The cultivation of the plants in rows, their mutually beneficent associations, the height of the vines, the soil and the manure, all help to insure the quality of the numerous appreciated wines that come from the region around Montpellier and from the Biterrois, the Narbonnais, the Minervois, the Corbières, the Roussillon, the Var and the Durance. As a rule these wines are blended to meet the demands of the market, and, as with all associations based upon expediency, results are not always happy.

Since the four *départements* of the Gard, the Hérault, the Aude and the Pyrénées-Orientales provide more than half of France's total output of wine, it will be realized that the price variations on the Montpellier and Béziers exchanges are not insensitive to the search for quality, and these fluctuations are followed feverishly by the southern winegrowers, who for a long time have been aiming at mass production.

Moreover, this interest in quality is demonstrated by the fact that certain privileged regions, whose wines have earned well-deserved fame, have been admitted to the paradise of *appellations contrôlées.* This is so as regards wine from Cassis (rich, smooth reds, and very dry whites), the product of 271 hectares, arranged in terraces in a picturesque arena of limestone rocks. A little farther to the east, Bandol produces some estimable wines, and so does Bellet in the Niçois.

Passing from Provence into Languedoc, we find a number of vines growing from Mauzac stock on the gravel and limestone hillsides of Limouxin in the Aude, where the yield, using moderate pressure, does not exceed 1 hectoliter per 150 kilograms of harvested grapes. This wine—as the monks of the abbey of Saint-Hilaire discovered in the sixteenth century—when put into stone vessels in April, becomes spontaneously effervescent and sparkling; this is the famous Blanquette de Limoux, remarkable for its special bouquet. It is a pleasant, refreshing wine, but rather small, and perhaps more often likened to champagne by those who make it than by those who drink it.

The most striking proof, however, of the southern soil's ability to yield wines of quality is provided by the incomparable naturally sweet wines produced at Frontignan—right in the midst of Montpellier's *pinard*-producing areas—and also on a sizable area of the Pyrénées-Orientales extending as far as the Spanish frontier. These wines, which have a low yield to the hectare, and which are the product of noble vines—i.e. Muscat, Grenache, Macabeo and Malvoisie—stay naturally sweet without the addition of any foreign matter except a certain quantity of alcohol. With their inimitable bouquet, it is a pity they are not better known.

The stony and arid soil of the Hérault produces the Muscat of Frontignan, whose praises Rabelais sang, and which Voltaire believed to be instrumental in prolonging his life. The range of wines in the Pyrénées-Orientales is astonishingly rich. Stretching from the Spanish frontier to the coast at Argeles, the four communes of Cerbère, Banyuls, Port-Vendres and Collioure produce the naturally sweet wines of the Côte Vermeille—white, red and *rosé*—

and have the right to the *appellation* "Banyuls." The red, slightly fortified wines of the area are rich in iron, which can sometimes be tasted, and like port, they are frequently drunk as a dessert wine.

Inland, in the dry valley below the peaks of the Albeze and the Corbières, lies the village of Maury, whose sweet wines, the product of black-graped Grenache stocks that grow on the valley's shaly, scree-covered slopes—the land of lavender and juniper—are well known to the German wine importers. Near the sea, the Rivesaltes *cru* is grown on the French side of the Roussillon Pass, where the red soil is planted with Muscat and Malvoisie stocks. Indeed, the father of the region's most illustrious son, Marshal Joffre, was a Rivesaltes cooper.

It is between this celebrated winegrowing area and the Maury area that we find the Côtes d'Agly, which are barred to the south by imposing mountains seperating the valleys of the Têt and the Agly. There the arid slopes, planted with Grenache and Muscat stocks, provide the naturally sweet wines of the Côtes d'Agly, which are now produced by up-to-date cooperatives. To conclude, mention must be made of the Haut-Roussillon slopes, and of the stony soil of Aspres, which produce naturally sweet wines from Grenache, Muscat and Malvoisie grapes, as well as full-bodied red wines employed in the preparation of aperitifs.

WINES OF BURGUNDY

"The vineyards of Burgundy," writes Constantin-Weyer, "are by no means among the most spectacular, and great estates such as those of the Bordelais must not be looked for here, neither the châteaux nor even the farms. The winegrowers live as villagers and—yes, even today—clamber sturdily about the steep slopes with their baskets on their backs." So, traveling from the north to the south, let us explore this region blessed by the gods, whose very soil underlines the distinctions between Upper and Lower Burgundy.

LOWER BURGUNDY

This region, which has an area of some 14,000 hectares, is situated for the most part in the *département* of the Yonne, and particularly in the Auxerrois. Red and white wines are produced throughout the *département,* and it is above all famous for the dry white wines of Chablis, which are harvested on the hillsides of the Serein, in the Auxerre district. Twenty communes have the right to the Chablis *appellation,* and the wine is made exclusively from Pinot grapes grown on Kimmeridge clay. Chablis is perhaps the driest of all white wines, a characteristic that traditionally makes it the perfect accompaniment to oysters, and it is hard to think of a wine paler in color. Most white wines darken as they grow older, but not Chablis, which is still as pale when fully mature at six years or so as when first bottled. The district lies dangerously near the grapevine's northern limits, and in some years—notably 1945, 1951 and 1953—almost the whole vintage has been destroyed by frost.

Apart from the Chablis from the most noteworthy *crus,* other highly esteemed wines have the right to the *appellation "Bourgogne des environs de Chablis"* (Burgundy from the Chablis neighborhood), and farther north the Aube region produces white, *rosé* and red wines from Trois-Riceys grapes in the Bar-sur-Seine district.

UPPER BURGUNDY

On the right bank of the Saône, the grapevine is queen. It graces the gentle hillsides of the Beaujolais, it infests the steeper hills of the Mâconnais, and it covers the famous slopes of the Côte d'Or, which, according to Stendhal, "is only a little mountain, sunbaked and ugly, but at every moment one comes upon an immortal name."

To explore Upper Burgundy, let us start at Dijon, that ducal city famous for its mustard as well as for its wines, and travel south. The first part of our journey takes us through an area some forty miles long, and varying in width from 500 to 2,000 yards, where 4,000 hectares of vines unfold their verdant finery to the sun. At Chenove—once, but no longer, a great wine-producing center—can be seen a medieval wine-press said to be the largest in the world and called "Big Maggie" after Marguerite, Duchess of Burgundy. Then we come to Marsannay-la-Côte, which in recent years has started to make a *rosé* wine that is fast growing in popularity. Conchey comes next, and then we arrive at Fixin, where the first of the great wines are found, although they are little known. They are dark red in color, with a high alcoholic content, and a marked bouquet. They age well, and the best of them are very little inferior to all but the greatest Chambertin. At Brochon there is little to detain us, but soon we come to Gevrey-Chambertin, where is harvested what has been called the king of wines and the wine of kings. Moreover it was Napoleon's favorite wine, and he even took a supply of it with him to Moscow.

Morey-Saint-Denis, eclipsed by its overpowering neighbors, leads us to Chambolle-Musigny, the chosen motherland of another very great *cru*, and here is found the celebrated Clos-Vougeot, to which passing French regiments traditionally render military honors. The Clos lies in the shadow of the great castle built by Cistercian monks in 1551; the castle's historic wine-presses had a narrow escape at the end of the last war when Nazi prisoners confined here by the Americans attempted to burn them for firewood; fortunately the prison commandant learned of their intentions in time, and saved the presses. Wine from Clos-Vougeot has a distinctive bouquet, full and scented, and the wine itself well deserves its great reputation.

Next come the Echezeaux, heralding Burgundy's finest pearl: Vosne-Romanée, whose renown is inseparable from that of the Princes of Conti. After such splendors one is hard put to it to sing the praises of Nuits-Saint-Georges, that hospitable little town and important commercial center, which produces wines of the highest quality, famous for restoring the Sun King's faltering forces in 1680. The local historian, Courtépée, maintains that the Côte de Nuits produces Burgundy's best wines. The Premeaux vineyard has equal merit, but those of Comblanchien*

*This village was savagely destroyed by the Germans in 1944, together with nearly all its inhabitants.

and Coggoloin have less striking claims upon our attention. Then the Côte de Nuits gives place to a rugged landscape strewn with woods and quarries.

The Côte de Beaune starts at Ladoix-Serrigny, but it is at Aloxe-Corton, at the foot of what is rather pretentiously called "the Mountain," that some very great wines are found, notably the famous white wine Corton-Charlemagne. This wine, bearing the name of the vineyard's original owner, is a generous wine, golden in color and firm in flavor. It is exclusively the product of Chardonnay grapes, and there is a faint suggestion of cinnamon in its bouquet.

Pernand-Vergelesses comes next, with its outstanding red wine, while the picturesque township of Savigny-les-Beaune provides wines of extremely fine quality. Then we enter Beaune itself, incontestably the capital of Burgundy. It is a proud of its 533 classified hectares as it is of its magnificent Hôtel-Dieu, which, since 1443, has been maintained by the proceeds of the Hospice's famous annual wine auction. This takes place in the Hospice's great courtyard on the third Sunday of each november. Sale is by inch of candle,* and if prices run somewhat high the buyer can at least reflect that the profit goes to the sick and needy. Beaune wines incline to be much lighter than those we have just been discussing, and most of them mature early. On the other hand, the wines of Pommard,

*A form of sale by auction: a pin is put through a candle, perhaps half way down; when the candle burns down to this point, the bidding stops and the last bid before this wins.

although Beaune's immediate neighbor, are firmer and tend to keep better.

After Pommard's twin red-earth hills, sheltering the ancient stones of this charming village, comes Volnay, whose wine, on the authority of Jullien, is the most agreeable in all France, and many people have heard the saying: "*On ne peut être gai sans boire du Volnay*" ("You can't be gay without drinking Volnay"). Next door to Volnay we have Monthélie, whose wines are recorded as far back as the ninth century.

Auxey-Duresses, less well known, extends as far as the hillside of Meursault, a pleasant little township whose land, divided by a deep gorge, produces excellent red wine in the north and, in the south, "the best white wines in the world," which, although dry, are as mellow as could be wished; the stocks they come from are the famous Pinot Blanc and the Chardonnay. Below Meursault, we meet one of the greatest white wines, Montrachet—"divine Montrachet," it has been called. This is harvested at Puligny-Montrachet and Chassagne-Montrachet, which also produce red wines of quality. Sautenay, sheltered from the wind by a circle of hills, offers the visitor the pleasant sight of ancient houses picturesquely grouped, and some red and white wines of good quality, although not to be classed as "great."

MÂCONNAIS

The Mâconnais vineyards, extending from Tournus to Romaneche, are also rich in famous *crus,* both red and white. If Tournus wines have lost the fame awarded them in the Middle Ages by the monks of the Abbey of Saint-Philibert, stocks of Viré, Lugny, Clessé and Chardonnay still provide wines that rival Chablis. In the neighborhood of Mâcon the red Gamay vines, lying snug in the valley bottoms, produce a wine that was cherished by Louis XIV, and their renown is considerable. Farther on, the terrain's contours grow sharper, and perched on the steep slopes we find the famous vineyard of Pouilly-Fuissé, which produces the magnificent pale gold wine of that name. This can be drunk quite young, and at the same time it keeps well. There is, it is true, a school of thought that maintains that Pouilly-Fuissé does not develop much after four or five years in bottle, but in my opinion its full quality is only attained after some twenty years, and that it will keep so long is not disputed.

Beyond the Pass we find ourselves on a granitic terrain planted with Gamay stocks: we have entered the Beaujolais country.

BEAUJOLAIS

Over an area of some 200 square kilometers, the Gamay stocks—bearing black grapes that yield a white juice—adorn the slopes of a beautifully molded terrain that produces wine of an incomparable freshness, precocious enough to be drunk young. This is Beaujolais, which is made exclusively from Gamay grapes, and although the Gamay is looked down upon elsewhere, here it comes into its own, and Beaujolais is the carafe wine that probably graces more tables in France than any other.

Between Saint-Amour and La Chapelle-de-Guinchay,

Upper Beaujolais prides itself on some famous *crus* Juliénas, Chenas and the notable Moulin-à-Vent, which is a little heavier than most Beaujolais. Next we come to Fleurie, with its full-flavored wine, Chiroubles, which is said not to travel well and is mostly consumed in France, and Morgon, whose wine keeps well and improves with moderate aging, and then we pass that towering lump of porphyry which is the Montagne de Brouilly. Brouilly, the wine, is extremely delicate, and there are some who maintain it should never be bottled, but drunk from the wood when two or three years old.

Farther south, on the way from Villefranche to Lyons, a host of localities follow one another, and these, if not so well known, nevertheless provide excellent table wines.

Indeed it is regrettable that a region so generously endowed has to be traversed so rapidly, but let us pay homage by repeating the words of Erasmus: "O beatific Burgundy, well may you be called the mother of men, whose breasts give such wonderful milk."

WINES OF THE CÔTES DU RHÔNE

Who is to say why the most notable vineyards prefer the slopes of the valleys that flank the great waterways? From Lyon to Avignon, the Rhône's two banks are in harmony in that they mark out the areas producing the excellent wines of the Côtes du Rhône. At the outset, 7 kilometers downstream from Vienne, we come to the ancient vineyard of Côte-Rôtie—the Roasted Slope—on the steep slopes on the right bank; this vineyard, which comprises the Ampuis and Tupin communes, is planted with Syrah and Viognier stocks, growing on a stony soil cultivated in terraces. The wine of the Côte-Rôtie, deep purple in color and having a subtle bouquet, is a great wine and a generous one, with an alcoholic content of 12° to 14°. Indeed, it is difficult to give preference to either of the two principal *crus*: Côte-Brune or Côte-Blonde. Farther south, we come to the Condrieu vineyard with its white wines from Viognier stocks, and, in the Verin commune, we find the Château-Grillet estate, which produces a remarkably luscious white wine that is too little known.

Now let us explore the Rhône's left bank and visit Crozes-Hermitage, with its red and white wines, closely related to those of Tain-l'Hermitage, some 20 kilometers north of Valence. Here, where the terraced vines form great steps whose granite soil can only be kept in place with difficulty, stocks of Syrah, Marsanne and Roussanne give red wines of a particularly rich color and some white wines just as generous, such as those of Mercurol, a satellite commune of the Hermtage.

Crossing the river again, we come upon Cornas, with its red wines; then, in a romantic setting near the ruined château of Crussol, we find Saint-Péray, whose dry white wine has been steadily growing in fame since the early part of the last century, when the champagne process was first applied to it to give it the desired effervescence. This elegant sparkling wine, with its light scent of violets, now has many devotees.

From Saint-Péray to Valence is only a step, and, as we ascend the valley of the Drôme, we find that the steep

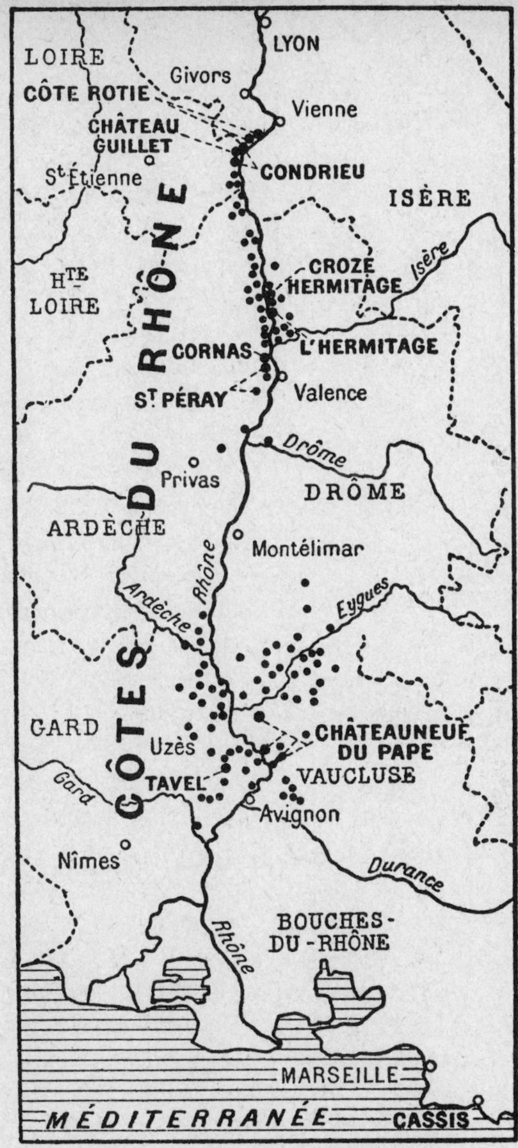

Fig. 3. Wines of the Côtes du Rhône

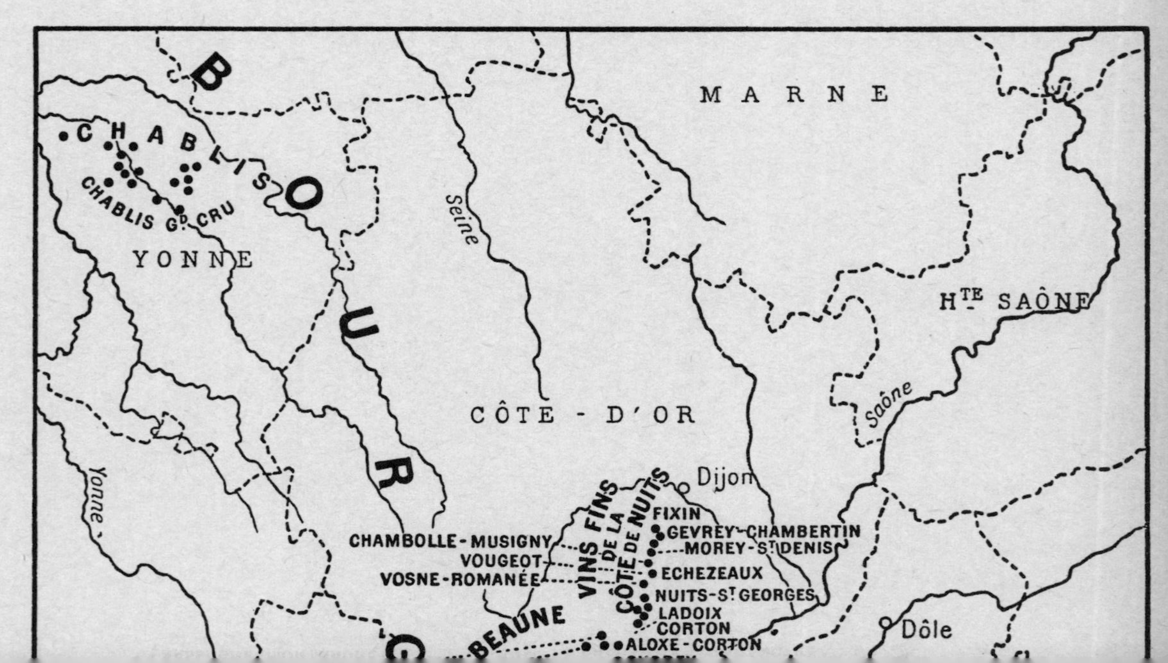
MARNE
Hte SAÔNE
Saône
Seine
CÔTE - D'OR
YONNE
Yonne
CHABLIS
CHABLIS Gd CRU
BOURG
Dijon
Dôle
VINS FINS DE LA CÔTE DE NUITS
FIXIN
GEVREY-CHAMBERTIN
MOREY-St DENIS
CHAMBOLLE-MUSIGNY
VOUGEOT
VOSNE-ROMANÉE
ECHEZEAUX
NUITS-St GEORGES
LADOIX
CORTON
ALOXE-CORTON
BEAUNE

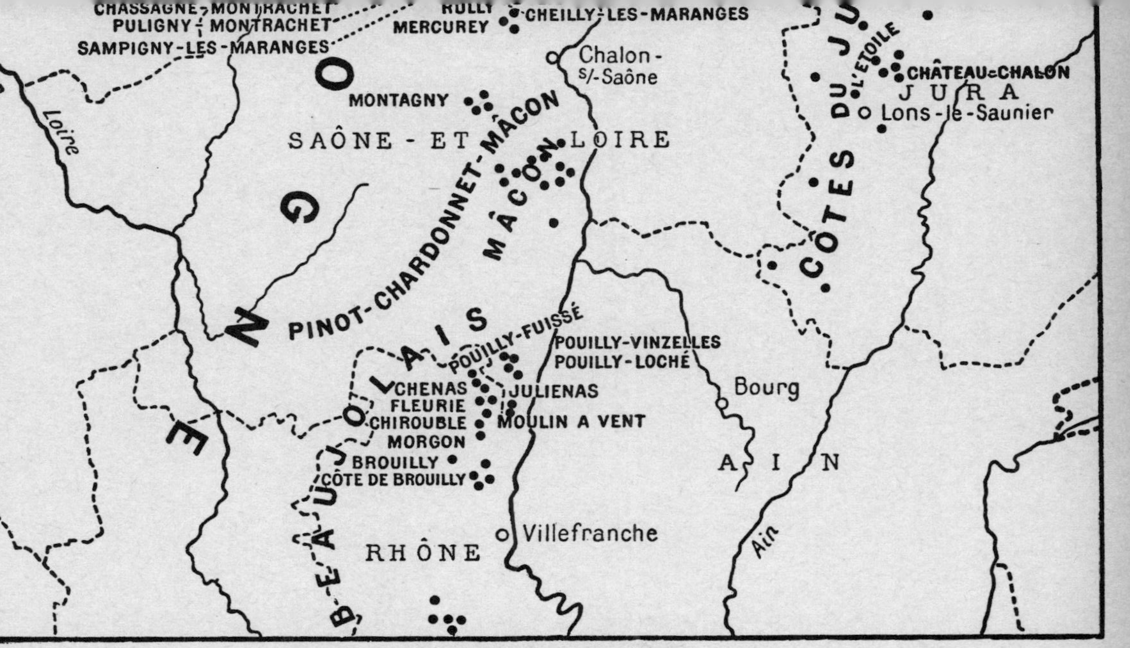

Fig. 4. Wines of Burgundy and the Jura.

slopes flanking the river are planted with Clairette and Muscat stocks; and, from Saillans to Die, the Clairette de Die has been made since that distant past when Roman emperors honored it as the wine of the Dea Augusta. Today this light, agreeable wine—rendered spontaneously effervescent by repeated filtering—enjoys little more than local renown, which is a pity, since it is to be preferred to the better known, but too elaborately processed, Asti Spumante from the other side of the Alps.

At Châteauneuf-du-Pape, on the left bank of the Rhône, we enter Provence, with its pebbly soil of alpine diluvium planted with thirteen different stocks. The popes were certainly wrong to leave these favored regions, with their floods of liquid gold and rubies.

A final crossing of the Rhône, and we enter the Gard, the country of the *rosé* wines. The pretty village of Tavel and, less well known, that of Ledenon, offer remarkable wines, to be drunk young and fresh. Tavel's excellent *rosé* is particularly suitable for export, since it has a high alcoholic content, which insures that, unlike most *rosés*, it travels well. This was the drink of the troubadours, Paul de Cassagnac has criticized it severely as producing a sensation of hoarseness!

WINES OF BORDEAUX

Nowhere in the world can a wine-growing region be found endowed with greater prestige than that located on the marches of Bordeaux, an incomparable grouping of vineyards whose praises were sung by the poet Ausonius as early as the fourth century. "My vineyards overhang the

Garonne's yellow waters," he wrote, and, after sixteen centuries, the passion of the people of the Bordelais for the grapevine remains unchanged. "The lasting splendor of the Bordelais *crus,*" wrote Constantin-Weyer, "is owed to the feudal regime, which bred and cultivated a tradition of great wines." The seigneurs, in seeking to rival each other, fostered the spirit of emulation to a point where profit-seeking was forgotten in the desire to produce wonderful wines, which were given away rather than sold; and after all, who could possibly pay a price commensurate with the loving and intelligent care lavished over so many years upon the grapevines of the Bordelais? When, in the Sauternes country, we see the crop harvested literally grape by grape, we can only take off our hats to those tireless and dedicated workers toiling thus out of pride in their work. Although it is the wines of commercial quality that have brought fortune to Bordeaux—and the prosperous activity of the famous Chartrons district bears witness to this—the foundations were laid by disinterested labor, and never have rewards been better deserved.

From whichever point we enter the region, we see signs of the wonderful product of a beautiful countryside as it makes its enchanted way from vine to cellar. Rather than lose ourselves in a mere literary description, let us start our tour of exploration by impressing the traveler's memory with the place names that indicate the wine-growing regions' principal divisions, and he can change their order to suit his convenience: Médoc—Graves—Sauternes—Entre-deux-mers—Saint-Emilionnais. Although, as Jullien points out, "All Bordeaux wines have qualities in common that indicate their origin," each region has its own characteristics, and it is these that the traveler will want to take note of.

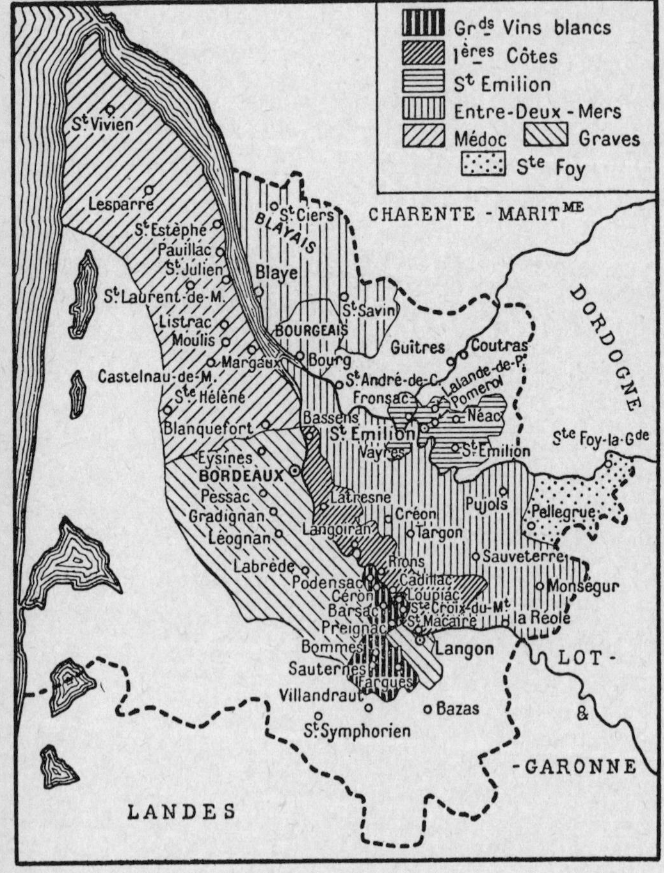

Fig. 5. Wines of Bordeaux

MÉDOC

The Médoc borders the left bank of the Gironde and the upper reaches of the Garonne; over an area some 80 kilometers long and 5 to 10 kilometers wide, lying between Soulac and Blanquefort, it displays an uninterrupted belt of vines drawing products of world-wide fame from an impoverished and flinty soil. Since 1855 these wines, magnificently light, and with a fine bouquet, have been classified in five categories of major *crus,* and these are succeeded by a host of lesser yet highly esteemed *crus* for everyday drinking, the complete list of which would run to many pages.

The stocks, mostly Cabernet, Sauvignon, Carmenère, Malbec and Verdot, are very low-growing and pruned to a cruciform shape; the grapes are harvested in the second fortnight of September. Then, in the château's long, low wine-sheds, known as *chais,* an extensive series of routines are undertaken that, covering several years, finally produce an astonishing range of red wines with an alcoholic content of 9° to 12°.

The boundary line between the Médoc and the Haut-Médoc is to be found at Saint-Seurin, and the central point of the Haut-Médoc is at Moulis-en-Médoc, on a line of hills. Farther to the north, and bordering the Gironde, is Saint-Julien, land of octogenarians; here grow some 450 hectares of vines. Next door is Pauillac, the Médoc's capital, and here, on 765 hectares, are grown the greatest *crus* providing the famous Château clarets: Lafite-Rothschild, Latour, Mouton-Rothschild, Pichon-Longueville, Duhart-Milon, Pontet-Canet, etc. At Saint-Estèphe, 1000 hectares of vine annually produce ten to fifteen thousand hogsheads of wine. It is sad that we cannot mention, for want of space, the notable wines from the communes of Margaux, Cantenac, Soussans, Labarde, Arsac and Saint-Laurent.

GRAVES

The Graves region, next door to the Médoc, covers an area some 50 kilometers long and 15 to 20 wide, and its vineyards splendidly encircle the city of Bordeaux. Then it continues toward the south between the majestic Garonne and the forests and, toward its southern extremity, embraces the Barsac area. The shallow soil, which is sandy where not pebbly, produces admirable wines, both white and red, and the latter are as well-bred as those of the Médoc. The required minimum alcoholic content is 10° for the claret and 12° for the white wine. Among the white wines made at Pessac, which is a suburb of Bordeaux, is the outstanding Château-Haut-Brion; although this vineyard has been famous for red wines since medieval times, it was not until some sixty years ago that it seriously started to produce white wine. At first the experiment was not very encouraging, but in the thirties the soil was given a six-year rest and then replanted. The experiment was fantastically successful, as anyone who has tasted the vintages of 1945, 1947, 1949 and 1953 must know. Like most Bordeaux wines, Château-Haut-Brion, both red and white, keeps for decades, and is an excellent investment for those starting cellars. Also at Pessac is the vineyard of the Château-Pape-Clement, planted by the first of the Avignon popes, whose name it bears. The Château-la-Mission-Haut-Brion at Pessac-Talence also has spiritual connections, for it was here that Saint Vincent, the patron saint of winegrowers, got drunk and was turned to stone by way of punishment. He stands there still, grasping a battered bunch of grapes with his miter at a rakish angle. At Talence, on the other side of the railway, is the Château-La-Tour-Haut-Brion, and a few kilometers to the south we come to Leognan, where is situated the Château-Haut-Bailly, producing noteworthy red wine. Saint-Pierre-de-Mons, to the east of Langon, produces white wines of an exceptional quality.

SAUTERNES

The Sauternes region is on the right bank of the Ciron, a tributary of the Garonne, and although its extent is small (it comprises no more than the five communes of Sauternes, Bommes, Preignac, Barsac and Fargues), its renown is great as the home of an incomparably famous sweet white wine, extremely luscious, and with a remarkable bouquet. On a soil that is white clay in places and gravelly sand in others, Semillon, Sauvignon and Muscadelle stocks are expertly cultivated in a manner peculiar to the region, since the grapes are left on the vines until they are extremely ripe and start to shrivel. By this means a natural concentration of must is induced, a process that is curiously accelerated by the appearance of *Botrytis cinerea.* Slowly the grapes wither and their color changes from a purplish-brown to a very dark red; the gathering of the grapes is carried out in a number of stages with minute care, the pickers going over the vines a dozen times or more to find grapes at just the right stage of rottenness. Consequently harvesting the grapes is a slow process, lasting eight to ten weeks, and in some places it has been known to last until Christmas. Production rarely exceeds 900 liters to the hectare, but how wonderful are these wines whose great *crus* are the celebrated Château-d'Yquem, from the parish of Sauternes (which, in the sixteenth century was owned by the Eyquem family, that of the essayist Montaigne), Château-Rieussec from the parish of Fargues, and Château-Climens from Barsac. For more than a century, Château-d'Yquem has been considered the greatest dessert wine in the world, unequaled both in the delicacy of its fragrance and the richness of its flavor.

Opposite Sauternes, overhanging the Garonne's right bank, the rocky slopes of Sainte-Croix-du-Mont provide a magnificently extended panorama, and here 9,000 to 12,000 hectoliters of wine, very similar to Sauternes, are harvested annually, while the neighboring parish of Loupiac prides itself upon rich wines of comparable quality. Mention, too, must be made of Cérons, with 800 hectares of vines; nor should Podensac be left out.

ENTRE-DEUX-MERS

It would be more appropriate to call this region "Between-two-rivers" than "Between-two-seas," since the spur of land producing these white wines, some sweet and some dry, lies between the Garonne and the Dordogne. The soil is fertile, and yields are relatively high, particularly in the low-lying parts. Numerous cooperative wine-producing plants have been set up, and so the winegrowers are aided by the most up-to-date equipment.

At the region's eastern end, bordering the Dordogne, is the Sainte-Foy-Bordeaux area stretching toward Sainte-Foy-la-Grande, while toward the western point, between Bordeaux and Libourne, a tiny enclave of gravel soil called Graves-de-Vayres provides very agreeable red and white wines after two years in cask.

SAINT-EMILION

Now we cross the Dordogne to enter a noted region where the famous Saint-Emilion wines, grown on white-clay slopes, are harvested. The fine stocks providing them are Bouschat, Cabernet, Merlot and Malbec. Mention must be made of the following communes: Saint-Emilion, Saint-Christophe-des-Bardes, Saint-Hippolyte, Saint-Etienne-de-Lisse, Saint-Laurent-des-Combes, Saint-Pey-d'Armens, Vignoret and Saint-Sulpice-de-Faleyrens; and there are a few more also entitled to the "Saint-Emilion" *appellation*. Almost every commune is named after a saint, and in no other corner of the earth is hagiolatry so agreeably observed as in this one. Moreover the lovely little town of Saint-Emilion has two particular amenities: a wishing stone on which the saint slept, and a match-making well; if a girl throws two hairpins into it and they form a cross at the bottom, she will be married before she is a year older!

Pomerol, not far from Libourne, completes the Saint-Emilion vineyards. It has 624 hectares of white-clay soil, producing wines of great delicacy that are not unlike certain Burgundies.

The Côtes de Fronsac, set picturesquely in a rolling countryside where the waters of the river Isle meet those of the Dordogne, produce red wines that soon take on a topaz tint, and the Côtes-Canon have some highly esteemed *crus,* which are the product of some 400 hectares of vines in the parishes of Fronsac and Saint-Michel-de-Fronsac.

Opposite Pomerol, Lelande-de-Pomerol produces some sweet wines that are soon ready for bottling. Finally, Meac, an outpost of Saint-Emilion, annually produces 10,000 hectoliters of a full-bodied wine with a marked bouquet. The Premières Côtes de Bordeaux, on the Garonne's right bank, comprise about a dozen communes producing red wine, of which the most productive are Quinsac, Camblanes Saint-Caprais-de-Bordeaux, Cambes and Cenas.

On the Gironde's right bank, opposite the Médoc region, lies the Blayais, and the red and white wines of the Côtes de Blaye are much in demand for export. Also, mention must be made of the wines of Sainte-Foy-Bordeaux, on the borders of the Gironde and Dordogne *départements.*

We shall end our survey of the province—which includes huge areas with the right to the simple *appellation* "Bordeaux"—by pausing at Bourgeais, whose clayey hillsides dominate the confluence of the Dordogne and the Garonne. Here are harvested red table wines, light in character, as well as white wines (dry, semi-dry and sweet), which, rich in vitamins, are known as "medicinal wines"; these are ready to be bottled after no more than two or three years in cask.

WINES OF THE SOUTHWEST

The nearness of Bordeaux in no way eclipses the merits of the region we shall now explore, which can be pleasantly traversed by following the course of the Dordogne.

At Lamothe-Montravel we enter what has been called "Montaigne's Wine-store," but surely the author of the *Essays* was gourmand rather than a gourmet when he wrote this about the local wine: "To drink little and moderately

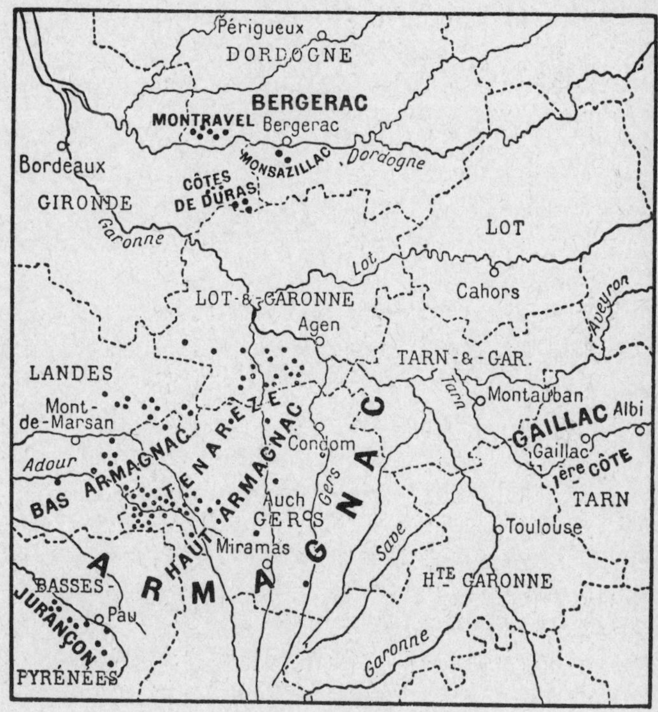

Fig. 6. Wines of the Southwest and Armagnac

and at mealtimes only is to ration God's favors." Yet, indeed, it is not easy to resist the charms of the white wines of Montravel, some mellow and others full-bodied, and the region's heady red wines have the right to the *appellation* "Bergerac"—this, of course, was the home town of Cyrano, he of the remarkable nose. Bergerac's white wines, the product of Semillon and Muscadelle stocks, are agreeable if somewhat small, and at one time they used to be sold in Paris almost before they had left the wine-press, under the unexpected name of "Macadam."

The region's special jewel, lying to the south of Bergerac, is the Monbazillac vineyard, which adorns the slopes of the Dordogne's left bank. Monbazillac, Pomport, Colombier, Rouffignac and Saint-Laurent-des-Vignes all produce very rich, full-bodied wines, mostly from Muscadelle stocks, but with some Sauvignon stocks as well. The grapes are harvested late in the year, after the appearance of *Botrytis cinerea,* and the wine's careful fermentation has to be arrested at a given point. Thanks to Huguenot emigrés, after the revocation of the Edict of Nantes, these magnificent wines found their way to Holland, and after more than two centuries this favorable trade is still maintained.

Farther to the south, the Côtes de Duras, which dominate the Dropt's green valley, are proud of their white wine, moderately sweet. One hundred and fifty kilometers from Bergeracois as the crow flies, the river Tarn divides the Gaillac region into two unequal parts; this region is particularly famous for its naturally sparkling wines. The vineyards are planted with Mauzac stock, and the chalk hillsides of the Tarn's right bank produce sweet Gaillac I^{res} Côtes, while the dry Gaillac I^{res} Côtes grows on the granitic soil of the Tarn's left bank. The dry white wines are not of great merit, but the sparkling Gaillac deserves mention, since no extra sugar is added to induce the effervescence, and the process employed calls for a period of aging in the *chais* when the bottles are stacked horizontally on shelves for several weeks before being dispatched. These wines, in spite of being sweet, have a marked bouquet and characteristics that make them well worth sampling.

Next, crossing a large part of Armagnac where there is nothing to detain us, we come to Béarn, where the famous Jurançon wine is produced. Here, local stocks—the Petit-Manseng, the Gros-Manseng and the Courbou—are trained on poles, growing on various soils in areas sometimes fairly inaccessible. The grapes, which are very small, are left on the vines for a considerable time, allowing the juice to concentrate until the middle of November, when, if the weather is humid enough, the mold *Botrytis cinerea* makes its appearance; in dry years the harvest is sometimes delayed until the middle of December. The yield is low, 18 to 25 hectoliters to the hectare, but the wine is a generous one with an alcoholic content of 11° to 15°, and its natural sugar insures that it is pleasantly sweet. Indeed, the King of Navarre knew what he was doing when he put a little of this wine on the lips of the future Henry IV the day he was born. Amsterdam and Hamburg have been buying Jurançon wines for a long time, and since the nineteenth century these wines have been selling in America and Belgium as well; but production is too small to sustain any considerable export trade. It is regrettable that this wine, which keeps so extremely well, is becoming unobtainable in France, as is its cousin from the Jura, Château-Chalon.

WINES OF THE LOIRE AND THE CENTER

The Loire and its tributaries are flanked by vineyards just as delightfully as are the Rhône and the Garonne. From the Central Plateau to the Atlantic more than 200,000 hectares of vines provide an astonishingly varied range of wines—table wines and vintage wines—whose true worth is becoming steadily better known.

WINES OF AUVERGNE

The transformation of Clermont-Ferrand into a great industrial metropolis has dealt a severe blow to the local vineyards, whose 25,000 hectares, principally planted with Gamay stocks, grace the most northerly spurs of the Auvergne chain, particularly in the Veyre and Vic-le-Comte cantons. The inhabitants of Puy-de-Dome think extremely well of Chanturgue's fresh and full-flavored wine, which has been compared to a lesser Bordeaux.

WINES OF THE ALLIER

Here the vineyards cover some 10,000 hectares, and hold their own against industrialization. Consequently the faithful devotees of *La Source de l'Hôpital* and other Vichy waters can pleasantly enliven their cures and activate their livers by appraising the local wines, and what more agreeable diuretic is there than the dry white wine of Saint-Pourçain, which has been widely compared to the Moselle wine, Zeltinger? Chantelle and Deneuille, on the Bouble's slopes, produce excellent red wines, fresh and richly flavored. Creuzier-le-Vieux, not far from Vichy, provides some wines that are rather more acid, but for which the author, a native of the region, has the same tenderness as his compatriots.

WINES OF THE NIÈVRE

In spite of its altitude, the Nièvre has some 5,000 hectares of vines. A few kilometers downstream from Nevers, the well-known vineyard of Pouilly-sur-Loire (with 1,300 hectares of Sauvignon and Chasselas stocks) produces a white wine that in flavor is comparable to hock. Of even better quality is Pouilly-Fumé—not to be confused with the Pouilly-Fuissé we have already met in Burgundy—and this recalls certain of the Sancerre wines. Although it is produced entirely from Sauvignon grapes, which are used in Bordeaux for sweet wines, it is a light, dry, clean-tasting wine, and it is said that Marie Antoinette had a particular fondness for it. Wine, both red and white, is also produced in the neighborhood of Cosne, and although the latter is quite unpretentious, it is much appreciated as an antidote to the nauseous waters of the little spa of Pougues.

WINES OF THE BERRY

In this region the vine makes its appearance at Argenton-sur-Creuse, serves honorably at Saint-Marcel, La

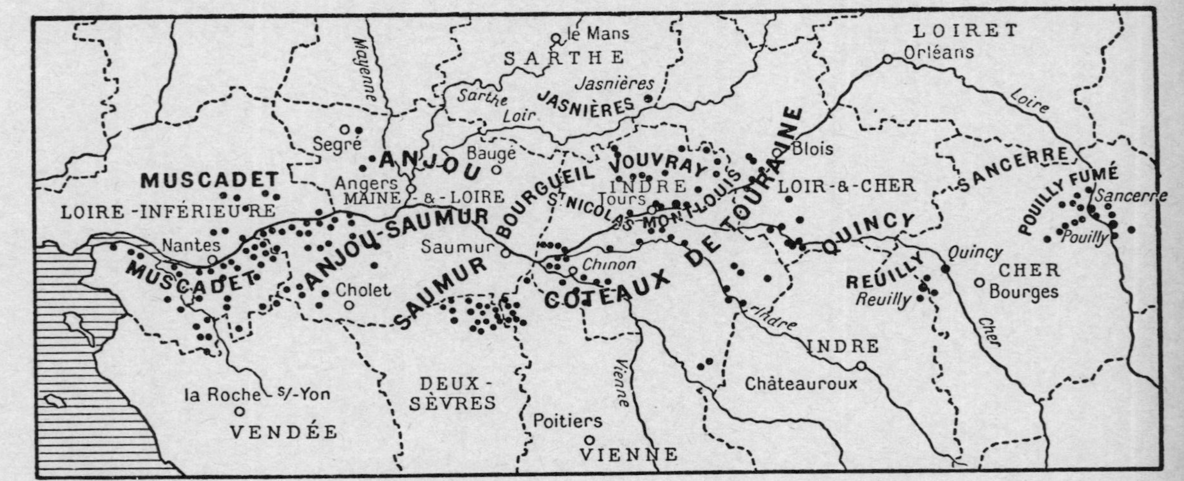

Fig. 7. Wines of the Center and the Loire

Châtre and Chateaumeillant, then achieves nobility at Quincy, Brinay and Reuilly, where 220 hectares of Sauvignon stocks grow on the impoverished soil of a chalky plateau. Sancerre—overlooking the Loire Valley almost opposite Pouilly-sur-Loire—displays its vineyards unostentatiously; they comprise a number of communes, of which the most famous is Chavignol. Red wines of good quality are produced from Pinot and Gamay stocks, while the important white wines are produced from 850 hectares planted with Sauvignon stock. These dry white wines, while not as distinctive as Pouilly-Fumé, have a clean freshness in common with it; but they keep badly and should be drunk young. Delightful *rosé* wines are also produced, but they are bad travelers, and the same can be said of the full-bodied red wines from Gamay grapes that are produced in the neighborhood of Bourges.

WINES OF THE LOIRET

The 10,000 hectares that constitute the Loiret's vineyards are divided into two groups: the Giennois area, where at Gien and Briare are produced red wines almost identical with those made in the neighborhood of Cosne; and the Gatinais area—land of honey and saffron—where white wines that keep well are produced from Gros-Meslier stocks. Although a century ago Brillat-Savarin praised the wine of Orléans, nowadays the vine flourishes there with no other ambition than to furnish the light and acid wines that form the raw material for the making of wine vinegar, an important local industry. Acetification takes place in half-full oaken casks piled one upon another, and the vinegar obtained has a bouquet such as malt vinegar can never hope to achieve. This industry, which owes much to Pasteur, provides a wonderful example of adaptability, by converting diseased yeast into a wholesome food product.

WINES OF THE LOIR-ET-CHER

The Sologne extends into Loir-et-Cher, occupying that half of the *département* where 25,000 hectares of vineyards flourish. The Sologne wines are dry and white, while around Blois (where the vine is declining) good red table wines are produced, and in the Vendomois we find the white wines of Troo, Montoire, Naveil and Villiers-sur-Loir, where the wine cellars are hollowed out of the solid limestone. As we descend the Loire, mention must be made of La Chartre, Marçon and the Coteaux de la Dème and the Clos des Jasnières.

WINES OF TOURAINE

As a traveler enters Touraine—the Garden of France —he is at once struck by the beauty of the countryside, which boasts 35,000 hectares of vines growing on chalkland molded by the Loire and its tributaries. It is in this region that we find those curious dwellings tunneled into the rock that shelter an important number of troglodytic wine-growers. In this region wines abound—those of commercial quality, as well as the great wines—and they are now classified in five categories.

The first category comprises the great red wines with *appellation contrôlée,* produced from Cabernet stocks.

"How good God is to give us this good wine," said Rabelais, who was born at Chinon, which shares with Bourgueil the honor of producing the great wines. Saint-Nicolas-de-Bourgueil, on the boundary between Touraine and Anjou, has vines growing on gravel soil and others on white clay chalkland, while Bourgueil itself, perched on a hillside three miles or so from the Loire, produces wine "for intellectuals," according to Jules Romains; it recalls the wines of the Médoc, with a hint of astringence and a subtle scent of strawberries. As for Chinon, its renown is by no means negligible, and it gives its *appellation* to many communes: Ligré, Cravant, Les Coteaux, Huismes, Le Roche-Clermault, Savigny-en-Véron, Panzoult and Avoine. Connoisseurs note a particular bouquet in Chinon wine, recalling the scent of violets, and Rabelais celebrated "this good Breton wine, which is not produced in Brittany, but in the fine country of Véron," the point being that locally the Cabernet vine is known as the "Breton," not because it originally came from Brittany, but because it was sent from Bordeaux to the Abbé Breton.

The second category comprises the great white wines of Vouvray and Montlouis. Only one variety of vine is cultivated and, as with Sauternes, it is harvested late, after the appearance of *Botrytis cinerea*. The wine produced at Vouvray and in the less well known communes of Rochecorbon, Vernou, Sainte-Radegonde, Chancay, Noizay, Reugny and Parcay-Meslay is rich and velvety, but it does not travel really well, although it can attain an alcoholic content of 13°. Some of the white wines produced on the Loire's other bank, at Montlouis, Lussault and Saint-Martin-le-Beau, are allowed to mature normally, and the champagne process is applied to them to produce a sparkling quality that is much esteemed.

The third category comprises wines having the right to the *appellation contrôlée* "Coteaux de Touraine," and the fourth comprises *rosé* wines produced from Cabernet, Gamay and Groslot stocks; these wines, entitled to *appellation contrôlée,* are much appreciated for their freshness.

Finally, the fifth category consists of red table wines, pleasantly full-flavored and produced from Cot, Gamay and Groslot stocks.

WINES OF ANJOU

For the most part the vineyards of this charming countryside lie to the south of the Loire. Anjou is known, above all, for its white wines, luscious and highly alcoholic, produced after over-ripening from Pinot or Chenin grapes. This wine should "glisten" in the glass, that is to say, it should sparkle lightly, without really effervescing. Anjou also produces light dry wines that are used for the making of the well-known sparkling wines of Saumur, in a process that succeeds particularly well in the wine cellars of Saint-Hilaire-Saint-Florent. The red wines, velvety and full-flavored, from pure Cabernet stocks and from Cabernet-Sauvignon, rival those of Bourgueil and Chinon.

Let us start with the Saumur area. The slopes of Saumur comprise the Côte de Saumur and the Côte du Thouet, regions where the vine is mixed with other crops at Brézé, Chacé-Distré, Varrains, Souzay, Montsoreau and Dampierre-sur-Loire. Between the Loire and the Layon, we follow the course of the Aubance, and come to Quincé, Vauchrétien, Saint-Mélaine, Soulaines, Saint-Saturnin, Saint-Jean-des-Manouts, Guigné and Mure, all ancient fiefholds of the Château de Brissac, whose seigneur used to receive "cakes and famous wine" three times a year from the Prior of Saint-Mélaine. Today the Coteaux de l'Aubance produce two kinds of wine: the strawberry-scented *rosé* from Gamay and Cabernet stocks, and some "liqueur" wines that, although rich, are drier than those of the Layon.

This charming river flows into the Loire after passing below the Coteaux du Layon, home of Anjou's greatest wines, all rich in "liqueur" to a greater or lesser extent; these are produced from the Chenin Blanc. The grapes are left on the vines until the onset of *Botrytis cinerea,* and the over-ripening continues into November. The wine is drawn off in January or February, and it is bottled during the spring following the harvest, with the result that the grapes' full flavor is preserved, and a few years of aging in bottle are enough for the wine to reach its peak. The wines are sweet and full-bodied and especially noteworthy is the wine from the Quart de Chaume, which, in spite of its high alcoholic content, has a marked bouquet and a most agreeable lightness. There is so much poetry in the names of the communes of this region that it is a pleasure to say them over: Chalonnes, Chaudefonds, Saint-Aubin, Saint-Lambert, Beaulieu, Rablay, Faye, Champ-Thouarcé, Chavagnes and Martigné.

A little beyond Angers, and quite close to the river, are the Coteaux de la Loire, whose white wines, rather dry and pleasantly full-flavored, require several years in bottle. It is to them that the following communes owe their fame: Savennières, Bouchemaine, La Possonnière, Saint-Georges-sur-Loire, Saint-Germain-des-Prés, Champtocé, Ingrandes, Montjean and Pommeraye.

If we ascend the Sarthe and the Loire we come to the Coteaux du Loir and the Coteaux de la Sarthe, the homes of white wines of considerable quality, those of the first-named region being rich in "liqueur" while those of the second-named are dry; these wines can be placed midway between the Saumur wines and those of the Coteaux du Layon. The Coteaux du Loir also produce red and *rosé* wines, and although the red cannot really be recommended, the *rosés* are delightful. Finally, the vineyards of the Nantes area pride themselves on their Muscadet. It is a dry wine, unrivaled in its class, and its yellow color has a faint tinge of green. It is excellent for drinking at the start of a meal, and it goes extremely well with oysters. It is the only Breton wine to be classified and it is produced from Muscadet stock in three regions with *appellation contrôlée*: *Muscadet de Coteaux de Savre et Maine, Muscadet des Coteaux de la Loire* and, rather longwindedly, *Appellation départementale correspondant à l'ancien Comté de Nantes.*

WINES OF CHAMPAGNE AND OF THE EAST

WINES OF CHAMPAGNE

While full recognition must be paid to the means by which wine-growing and wine-making have been tirelessly perfected in Burgundy, Anjou and many other regions, it is nevertheless the Champagne region that furnishes the finest example.

Toward the end of the seventeenth century, Dom Pérignon, the blind cellarer of the Benedictine abbey at Hautvilliers, decided to use cork instead of cloth to seal the bottles in his charge, with the result, intentional or otherwise, that he imprisoned the carbonic gas formed during fermentation. Since then the directors of the great champagne concerns, inflexible traditionalists, have introduced no notable changes to the classical method of champagne-making. A sweet liqueur syrup is introduced into a bottle of dry wine of high quality, which then ferments slowly in its hermetically sealed glass prison to form carbonic gas. By placing the bottle neck downward, the fermentation's residue is made to collect against the cork, forming a thin layer of sediment that is quickly eliminated by a brief uncorking. The wine is recorked after the addition of some more liqueur syrup, intended to restore the effervescence and to provide the degree of sweetness demanded by the customer who, according to his humor, nationality or sex, likes his champagne to be either sweet, semi-dry, dry or extra-dry. Such, in very brief outline, is the champagne method, whose mysteries are performed in the heart of huge cellars, deeply tunneled into the region's limestone, a precaution taken by the commercial enterprises whose names guarantee the product's quality, without mention of the *crus* employed. It must be remembered that the whole process takes a number of years—five, six or even seven—and that the workers handling each bottle number between eighty and ninety.

With one exception, Champagne is the most northerly wine-producing region in the world, and one notable vineyard whose parcels of land, lovingly worked, are grouped around Rheims and Epernay, overlooks Champagne's dismal and barren plain from the sides of hills some five hundred feet high. The slopes of the Vesle's right bank, facing the south and the southeast, form the Petite-Montagne de Reims, with Hermonville, Saint-Thierry and

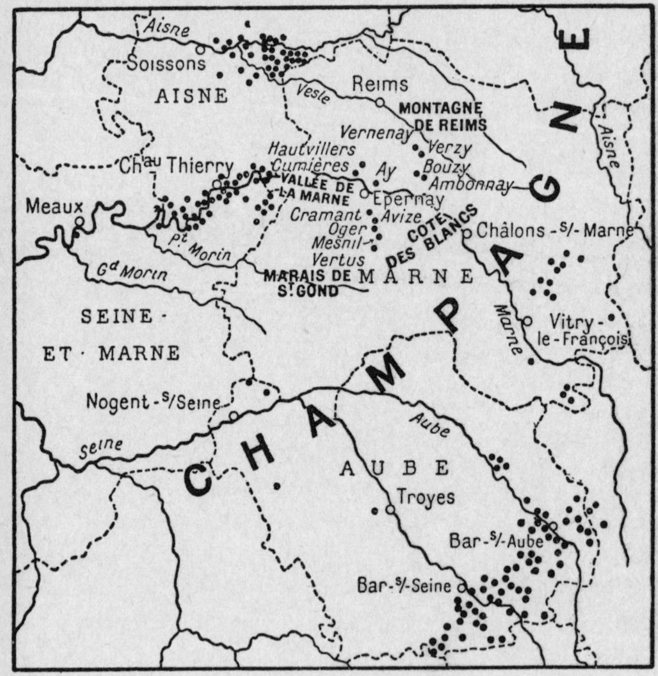

Fig. 8. Wines of Champagne

Trigny; those of the left bank, facing northeast and east, form the Grande-Montagne de Reims, and comprise Chamery, Rilly, Sillery, Mailly, Verzenay and Verzy. Farther south, two long ranges of hills follow the course of the Marne as far as Epernay; then each describes a wide arc, the one to rejoin the Grande-Montagne de Reims, and the other to make its way south. On the Marne's right bank we find Venteuil, Damery, Fleury, Dizy, Ay, Hautrillon, then Bouzy and Ambonnay, which, apart from white wines, also produce red wines as well-bred as the best Burgundies. The Marne's left bank forms the Côte-d'Épernay, with Vinay, Pierry and Moussy; then, on the arc formed by the Montagne d'Avize north of the Saint-Gond marshes, we find Cramant, Avize, Le Mesnil and Vertus.

The traditional method of cultivation on this impoverished and shallow soil is still often of the type known as *en folue*, or massed—50,000 to 60,000 plants to the hectare; the vines are trained on poles and pruned short, the pruning being carried out entirely by hand. Unskilled labor is used to carry the manure to the vines, transporting it in baskets carried on the back. The Pinot-Noir is favored by the Montagne de Reims and the Marne Valley; the Montagne d'Avize prefers the slightly later Chardonnay. The ordinary *crus* cultivate a variety of Pinot as being more resistant to frost.

A local committee names the day upon which the harvest is to start, and the price to be paid for the grapes is decided upon at the same time. The pressing is done by the big firms who buy the grapes from the growers. When the black grapes are pressed they are put through the presses at speed to prevent the skins impairing the color—that is, unless pink champagne is being made, in which case the juice and the skins are left together for a while. The wine is bottled in the spring following the harvest, but as we have indicated above, this is only the start of the process.

Indeed, a vast tome would be needed to describe the various phases of champagne-making that result in the production of these incomparable sparkling wines, known the world over by the names of the companies that make them. When next we see the wine sparkle lightly in our glasses, let us think of the incredible sum of ingenuity and labor demanded by a technique in which perfection is the rule, and let us remember that the winegrowers of Champagne have but a single aim: to preserve for champagne, in spite of economic vicissitudes, the resplendent prestige that only quality can give.

WINES OF THE JURA

The Jura mountain chain, fringed by gently sloping foothills, is graced by the vines that, in all, cover a third of the Jura *département*, so justly known as "the good country." To the north there are the vineyards of Arbois, that little town so loved by Henry IV; moreover it was at Arbois that Pasteur wrote his immortal *Etudes sur le vin*.

The district's famous wines—white, golden, and the red *pelure d'oignon*, so called from its particular shade of color, which is that of an onion-skin—are harvested at Pupillon, Montigny-les-Arsures, Mesnay and Les Arsures. There are also some highly esteemed sparkling wines.

Some 20 kilometers to the southwest we come to the Château-Chalon vineyard, overtopped by an impressive spur of rock. This vineyard, though small in area, is great in fame, for it is the home of a very rare phenomenon: heady, amber-colored wine with an incomparable bouquet that can be kept in bottle for a hundred years without deterioration. This is the Jura's celebrated *Vin Jaune* (yellow wine); for a start it is allowed to ferment in deep pits hollowed out of the rock. After fermentation it spends anything up to eight years in cask; old casks are used, ones that have become well soaked by previous generations of the wine. As the wine develops, a thick film of *mycoderma vini* forms on its surface, protecting it from the air, and the final result is an austere wine with a high alcoholic content; after several years in bottle it takes on a faint flavor of nasturtium that is much admired by connoisseurs. Before the invasions of the phylloxera, the Jura was also noted for its straw wines, but they have now all but vanished.

Seven kilometers beyond Château-Chalon we come to the township of Etoile, with its little vineyard of the same name. Here can be appreciated some white wines that grow on the slopes of Mont Genestat, and that are often made into sparkling wines. The rest of the Jura wine industry merits mention, since, under the *appellation* "*Côtes du Jura,*" it produces some fine red wines, some golden wines (these are typical products of Sauvagnin grapes, and should not be drunk until they are six years old) and some excellent sparkling wines.

WINES OF ALSACE AND LORRAINE

The three wars of 1870, 1914 and 1939 have shown the world what importance Germany attaches to the possession of France's eastern marches. Among the riches she coverts are 14,000 hectares of vines in Lower Alsace, 9,000 in Upper Alsace, and 5,000 in Lorraine, producing altogether nearly a million hectoliters of wine every year, a third of it being produced by the German crop.

The Alsatian vineyards occupy the hills overlooking the Rhine from Thann to Wasselone, and, almost exclusively, they provide white wines whose range is comparable to the best hocks. The grapes most favored are Riesling, Traminer and Silvaner, together with certain muscatels. Pruned to a pyramid shape, the stocks give very varied wines.

The Alsatian winegrowers are characterized by a strong communal spirit, which is just as well in view of the extreme partitioning of the vineyards. Few things are pleasanter than a visit to the Colmar wine exchange, rounded off by a wine-tasting at the famous "Maison des Têtes." As for the regional wine fairs—at Molsheim, Barr, Colmar, Ammerschwir and Ribeauvillé—they form picturesque manifestations of commercial activity.

In Lorraine light red wines predominate; those of Vic, Ancy, Ars and Jussy must be mentioned. Much akin are the wines from Meurthe-et-Moselle (Thiaucourt), from the Meuse (Pineau de Bar-le-Duc), and from the Mirecourt and Neufchateau districts of the Vosges.

WINES OF CORSICA

Although the favorite wine of Corsica's best-known son was Chambertin, the wines of his native island are by no means devoid of merit.

Understandably, there is a strong Italian influence. Most of the vines grown are Italian, and although the Malvoisie is cultivated—giving its name to a pleasant dry white wine produced in the Bastia area—the three most popular stocks are probably the Sciacarello, the Genovese and the Genovesella. Unfortunately the Corsicans are inclined to spoil their wines by adding *vino cotto,* which is unfermented grapejuice boiled to a syrupy consistency.

No very accurate records are kept, but the island's annual production is believed to be about 250,000 hectoliters, and the vine is cultivated over an area of about 8,000 hectares. The most extensive vineyards are those at Cap Corse, and the white wine is a good deal better than the red. It lacks consistency, however, and some of the island's *rosé* wines—notably those produced to the south of Bastia—taste uncomfortably like liquid Turkish Delight!

Without a doubt, the island's nearest approach to a great wine is the Patrimonio, which is one of the few Corsican wines that can be found on the mainland, particularly along the Riviera. It goes particularly well with bouillabaisse and all highly spiced fish dishes.

Corsican wines tend to be heady—something not always apparent at the time of drinking—and even the lightest of beverage wines should be treated with respect for the bandit it may conceal!

WINES OF NORTH AFRICA

Although Algeria, Tunisia and Morocco are now politically independent of France, no one would deny that the vineyards of these countries are really an extension of the French wine industry, and no doubt France will remain their best customer for many years to come.

ALGERIA

As regards Algerian viticulture, the French forsook the cautious restraints of a bourgeois economy, and became enterprising and vigorously productive. These qualities produced a wine industry that now constitutes Algeria's greatest wealth, and wine comprises nearly half that country's exports to France.

In 1850 Algeria had only 762 hectares of vines, but soon after the industry's feverish growth was brought about by the ravages of the phylloxera in the Midi. By 1883, 45,629 hectares had been planted; by 1889 this figure had more than doubled (96,624 hectares); and by 1900 it had almost trebled (135,719 hectares). At the present time some 390,000 hectares are under the vine, and the wine-growing areas occupy nearly 750 miles of the littoral between Nemours and La Calle, and extend inland to a depth of some 60 miles.

The vines cultivated are those from the Midi that give a high yield, and wine-making is highly industrialized. The production of beverage wines is principally aimed at, since, in a hot country, the delicate processes of fermentation are fraught with the possibility of error. In 1923 Prosper Gervais drew attention to the dangers of modeling

North African viticulture upon that of the Midi, and his advice has been most wisely followed.

TUNISIA

In this country some 30,000 hectares of vines were destroyed by the phylloxera, and a further 20,000 hectares were rendered sterile; and, as elsewhere, the only effective remedy was the grafting of the vines onto American roots. Moreover it was found expedient to abandon the productionof ordinary wines and to concentrate on the preparation of liqueur wines such as the famous Muscat de Carthage, together with the production of dessert grapes, dried raisins and the grape's non-alcoholic products.

That was the advice I gave my pupils in 1910 at the Tunis School of Agriculture.

MOROCCO

The Moroccan vineyards, which in 1919 hardly comprised 700 hectares, grew steadily for the next few years at the rate of 800 to 850 hectares a year, reaching a total of 9,500 hectares by 1930. Thereafter the rate of progress quickened, and by 1935 23,000 hectares were under the vine; while the production of wine, which was 40,000 hectoliters in 1922, and 200,000 hectoliters in 1930, rose to 440,000 hectoliters in 1933, and in the following year exceeded local needs by about 100,000 hectoliters. In succeeding years the annual surplus varied between 300,000 and 400,000 hectoliters, with the result that by 1956 stocks in hand had reached a fabulous total of 2¼ million hectolitres. By means of a drastic reversal of its economic policy,

Morocco joined the ranks of the exporter countries. By continuing to produce a mass of *pinard* she has taken a wrong turn; an effort ought to be made to develop wines of good quality.

CHAPTER 4

Eaux–de–Vie

Our survey of the wines of France would be incomplete if we passed over in silence those light and acid wines that are not very pleasant to drink, but that can be enhanced by distillation to an astonishing degree.

Two regions have brought the technique of making *eaux-de-vie* by the distillation of wine to a degree of perfection that cannot be surpassed, and when these spirits have undergone a long period of aging, they acquire a bouquet and a subtlety of flavor that is beyond description.

The names of these two regions, Charente and Armagnac, have been known the world over for a long time, and so firmly established is their fame that foreign imitators—and they are legion—do not hesitate to purvey their bottles of rotgut under labels copied from those of genuine French products. Since defense measures against this dangerous and dishonest practice have not proved very effective, it becomes paradoxically necessary to give exact details of how, in France, the great *eaux-de-vie* are made.

COGNAC

The outstanding characteristics of the Cognac countryside are a chalky soil and a mild climate. The region's vineyards, laboriously recovering from the ravages of phylloxera, are still a long way from their 1875 zenith, when there were 110,000 hectares under cultivation; now the figure is 72,000 hectares, shared between the *départements* of the Charente and the Charente-Maritime. The Folle Blanc is the stock mostly cultivated, and this has a high productivity, yielding up to 100 hectoliters to the hectare if not pruned short. In a good year the harvest will bring in nearly four million hectoliters of an acid wine with an alcoholic content varying between 7° and 11° and—it must be faced—with a fairly disagreeable taste. It was in the thirteenth century that the winegrowers of Charente, anxious to avoid the heavy cost of transporting wines, took to distilling them, and the resultant *eaux-de-vie,* called cognac ever since, revealed such marked quality that the use of the still quickly became general. Nowadays the operation consists of two successive heatings over a naked flame, the wine being "cooked" with its lees; the alcohol obtained should not exceed 72°. After aging for a long time in oaken casks, the liquor loses some of its alcoholic strength and takes on a beautiful golden-yellow hue, while the slow combining of its constituents, together with the action of the atmospheric oxygen, produces a bouquet of extreme delicacy, which recalls the scent of flowering vines. The addition of small quantities of sugar and caramel in the correct proportions, and the reduction of the alcoholic content by the addition of distilled water, result in the production of cognacs of a very consistent quality, whose selling prices vary according to age and the types of wine used as raw material.

Seven areas of production, whose boundaries were set

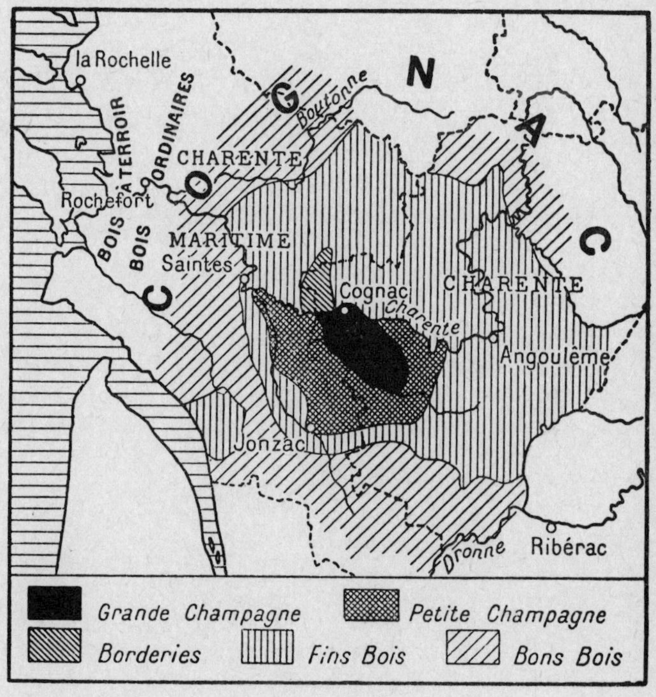

Fig. 9. Cognac

by official decrees in 1909, 1928 and 1938, are classified according to the quality of their product under the following names: (1) Grande fine Champagne and Fine Champagne; (2) Grande Champagne; (3) Petite Champagne; (4) Borderies; (5) Fins bois; (6) Bons bois; and (7) Bois ordinaire. The sizable capital sum represented by the stocks of cognac held in the storehouses at any one time forms one of Charente's greatest treasures, and provides the buyer with indispensable guarantees of quality, purity and origin.

It should also be pointed out that a *Mistelle* of high quality is produced in this region, by mixing fresh grape-juice with wine alcohol. The final product, with an alcoholic content of 18° to 22°, is called "Pineau des Charentes". It deserves to be better known, the more so since its origins date back to the sixteenth century.

ARMAGNAC

Armagnac, cognac's only serious rival, is still far from having the world-wide fame of the Charente product, and in any case it is produced in a much smaller quantity.

The grape cultivated in Armagnac is the Piquepoul, which grows on white-clay soil in a region comprising parts of the Gers, Landes and Lot-et-Garonne *départements*. The region is divided into several sub-regions: the products of Lower Armagnac, on the boundaries of the Gers and the Landes, are the most highly esteemed, and the countryside is one of hills overlooking wooded valleys. Farther east, the Ténarèze, a country of plains, stretches toward Lot-et-Garonne, and provides *eaux-de-vie* of good quality. Finally, the more scattered vines of Upper Armagnac produce some *eaux-de-vie* of a poorer quality than the other two areas.

MARC

With the curious exception of the Gironde region, *eaux-de-vie-de-marc* are produced wherever wine is produced, and those from Burgundy are the most esteemed. Marc is a spirit obtained by fermenting the grape refuse left in the presses after the wine has been drawn off; it has a very special flavor owing to the essential oils contained in the grapeskins, and to the empyreumatic products that result from the firing. These *eaux-de-vie* are allowed to age in oaken casks for a long period, and the winegrowers devote as much tender attention to them as the cidermakers devote to preparing Calvados. To award the palm to one or another of these excellent natural alcohols is childish: the distribution of diplomas is a game that the universities can well be allowed to monopolize.

THE QUALITIES OF AN EAU-DE-VIE

The storehouses where the spirits age are not always the paradises that they are at Cognac. Three essential virtues condition the quality of an *eau-de-vie*: its delicacy, achieved by the subtle combining of flavor and bouquet; its body, so characteristic of the best *eaux-de-vie*, which, when you put a drop on your tongue, do not produce burning sensations as do cheap spirits, but which give a subtle and delicately shaded flavor that unfolds deliciously over the palate; and, finally, its age, which by allowing the oxidization of certain elements, replaces the excessive vigor of young *eaux-de-vie* by the mellowness of maturity. It should be noted that bad *eaux-de-vie* are not improved by aging and, indeed, their defects are accentuated. Moreover, do not forget that an *eaux-de-vie* is intended to be drunk drop by drop, so to speak. Ignorant or hasty spirit-drinkers swallow mouthfuls at a time, and under these conditions the best cognacs and the finest armagnacs will burn the throat; and, as for the others, there is a serious danger of total combustion.

LIQUEURS

Although the best accompaniment to black coffee is cognac, perhaps in fairness some of the better-known French liqueurs should be mentioned.

Probably the oldest liqueur, with a history of some four hundred and fifty years, and certainly the most famous, is Benedictine, which is distilled at Fécamp. It is very aromatic and extremely sweet, so much so that it is often drunk blended with brandy. To settle arguments we will point out that the letters D.O.M. on the Benedictine label stand for *Deo optimo maximo,* which is the motto of the Benedictine order.

A liqueur that is reminiscent of Benedictine, although much drier, is Vieille Cure. It is distilled at Bordeaux on a basis of cognac, and it is reputedly good for the liver.

Another famous liqueur with monastic associations is Chartreuse, which for nearly three hundred years was made at the Grande Chartreuse Monastery near Grenoble. There are three types of Chartreuse; they are, in descending order of potency, White, Green and Yellow. The first bears the words "Elixir des Pères Chartreux" on its label, and it is alleged to be a certain cure for almost all minor ailments. Green Chartreuse is said to contain more than a hundred different ingredients, but since the recipe is the secret of only four monks, this is difficult to verify. Yellow Chartreuse, milder and much sweeter, was at one time known as the "ladies' liqueur." In 1901 the monks went into exile in Spain, and for nearly fifty years no genuine Chartreuse was made, but its manufacture was resumed with the return of the monks to Grenoble in 1948. Somewhat similar to Chartreuse is the Basque liqueur, Angelica, which comes in two varieties, green and yellow.

The best-known French curaçaos are Cointreau and Grand Marnier. The latter is sold under two distinct labels: *Cordon Rouge*, is more potent but not so sweet as *Cordon Jaune*. Cassis, when served neat, is classed as a liqueur. Its informing flavor is black currant, and the best Cassis comes from Dijon. Alsace is renowned for at least three liqueurs, all colorless and all matured in glass—Quetsch, which is distilled from plums; Kirsch, from black cherries; and Mirabelle, from the yellow plums of that name. Sloes are the informing flavor of Prunelle, which is made principally at Chalon-sur-Saône. Mandarine's informing flavor is tangerine oranges, and a lemon flavor can be discerned in Liqueur d'Or, which, like Danzig's Goldwasser, has flecks of gold-leaf suspended in it—harmless, tasteless but decorative. Gentiane, flavored with the powdered roots of the yellow gentian, is said to be an excellent stomachic. A favorite with the young is the sickly-sweet, aniseed-flavored Anisette, and also there is Parfait Amour, which, violet both in flavor and color, is as sentimental as its name.

Too numerous to mention individually are the syrupy-sweet *crème* liqueurs, but by far the most popular is Crème de Menthe, which is usually green, but can be colorless, and which really does seem to do something for the digestion after a heavy meal.

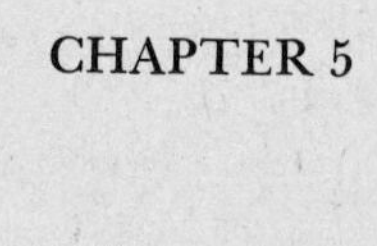

CHAPTER 5

Allied Industries

CORKS, GLASSWARE AND BARRELS

The answer to the question "Is God French?"—asked by the German writer F. Sirburg in a book that created a great stir—would appear to be yes, if the richness and variety of France's wine industry are anything to go by; but the extent of the gifts that Heaven has showered upon the French is even greater than is realized. The making of good wine requires exceptional skill and grapes of high quality, and those the French have; but, what is more, an enviable stroke of good fortune enables them to work entirely with products of their own soil as regards barrels, bottles and corks, and this self-sufficiency is certainly providential. The preservation, tending and aging of wine demands casks and barrels of good oak; the bottles must be stoppered with a cylinder of that elastic, insulating and imperishable substance that is cork; and the abundant supplies of cork on the Mediterranean shores of Provence and Mauritania constitute a priceless gift.

A cork oak will provide as many as ten or a dozen successive crops, representing a thickness of more than 15.8 inches of cork-bark—the wherewithal for the mass production of corks. Of course, the making of bottle-corks is of only minor importance among the increasing variety of uses that this amazing bark can be put to. Americans, who import this product from Portugal, have not failed to plant cork oaks in the Sacramento Valley, for the benefit of their own wine industry, and the use of cork is rigidly controlled while waiting for stocks to accumulate.

Since cork can be shaped to fit the necks of bottles, the shape and substance of the bottles themselves allow of a certain amount of variation. The ancient method of making bottles by hand is tending to disappear, which is just as well, since glass-blowing demands an exhausting physical effort on the part of the craftsman. Today there are some highly productive automatic machines that blow and gently mold the softened glass to make up to 2,000 bottles a day—a task that would demand thirty glass-blowers. In this instance it would be wrong to condemn the progress of mechanization.

The cylindrical, high-shouldered bottle is the rule for Bordeaux wines, while the wines of Burgundy, Champagne and Alsace are kept in bottles with sloping shoulders. As regards alcoholic drinks other than wine, a larger degree of fantasy is allowed, such as armagnac's squat gourd-shaped bottle, and the obsolete types of bottle affected by certain famous liqueurs. The Bordeaux bottle holds 75 centiliters, compared with the 80 centiliters held by the champagne bottle; it is interesting to note that the thick sides of the latter can withstand the pressure of six atmospheres. Sometimes wine of an exceptional vintage is put into bottles with two, three or more times the normal capacity, and these especially large bottles enable a particular wine to be shared among a large number of celebrators without risk of any discrepancy in quality—and sometimes the discrepancy between one bottle and the next is considerable, even though the wine has undergone exactly the same treatment in each case. For some reason that has never been properly elucidated, champagne bottles larger than the magnum (two bottles) are all named after personages from the Old Testament: a jeroboam holds four bottles, a rehoboam six bottles, a methuselah eight bottles, a salmanasar twelve bottles, a balthazar sixteen bottles and a nebuchadnezzar twenty bottles.

Drinking from the bottle without putting it to your lips is a picturesque practice, but hardly to be recommended even for the cheapest wine. In fact, before the wine is raised to the lips its color and clarity should be appraised, and its bouquet appreciated. "From glass to belly," says a famous song, and indeed metal drinking cups, although unbreakable and convenient for carrying around, as every soldier with his tin canteen knows, are not very gratifying to the lips even when made of silver or fine pewter. So, put your drinking cup in your pocket or on your table—it makes a perfect ashtray—and take a glass.

There is little to choose between crystal or ordinary glass, but the thickness of the glass must be taken into consideration. Yes, get rid of thick glasses, which require strength merely to lift them, and tolerate only clear, delicate glasses without engraving or decoration. Those glasses with the green or red cups that were once considered *de rigueur* for Alsatian and German wines may be pretty to look at, but they prevent your seeing the wine's color when you hold it up to the light, and that, indeed, was their original purpose—in the last century wine was often carelessly made, and the idea of serving white wine in colored glasses was to hide whatever impurities might be floating in it. As for the glass's shape, avoid one so standardized as to be dull, but bear in mind what is required of it—no risks must be run of splashing the tablecloth or your neighbors, yet you should be able to impart a gyratory movement to the wine to help you appreciate the bouquet, and this is hardly possible with a very shallow glass or a conical one. A cylindrical shape is more satisfactory, a slightly egg-shaped glass is excellent and a tulip-shaped one is perfect. Whichever you choose, keep it on the large side, and give the lie to Offenbach's celebrated verse:

Ce que je ne m'explique guère,
C'est pourquoi l'on boit à Paris
Le mouvais vin dans les grands verres,
Et le bon vin dans les petits.

(Just why I can hardly explain,
But when for wine in Paris I call
The bad wine comes in a big glass,
And the good wine comes in a small.)

Instead of serving quality wines in glasses of small capacity that have to be filled to the brim, use a glass of a size that needs never to be more than half-filled, and condemn out of hand those popular sayings whose false wisdom is poison to the mind, notably "My glass isn't big, but I can drown in my glass' (*Mon verre n'est pas grand, mais je bois dans mon verre*), and that other saying, no less absurd, "What does the bottle matter, as long as you get drunk?" (*Qu'importe le flacon pourvu qu'on ait l'ivresse*). On the whole, it is not advisable to smash the glass after drinking in the boisterous Russian manner, and in any case the washers-up will probably perform this ruinous operation for you. Incidentally, a whole industry has been organized to effect the mechanical washing and cleansing of bottles, which are kept in use until they crack or break. Although the bottle plays an indispensable part in the controlled aging of wines, this is only a continuation of a process that necessarily started with the wines spending several years in oaken casks.

Casks, barrels and butts! Indispensable containers where the wines spend their youth, sowing their wild oats, it might be said, by getting rid of undesirable sediment at each drawing off! Gradually the wine purifies, becomes limpid and brilliant, while at its heart subtle elemental combinations take place to form its bouquet. It is difficult to explain exactly why this astonishing chemistry, with its slow rhythm, only succeeds when the wine is enclosed in oak, but the porosity of the wood permits oxidization, and this in turn produces variation in atmospheric pressure, temperature and movement. These factors help explain the old practice, common in the days of sail, of taking wine "to the Indies and back" in order to mature it. However, as regards the aging of wine, it is useless to try to force nature's hand. The most modest wine of good quality ought to be kept in the wood for at least two or three years, periodically purified, filtered and drawn off, and in every way almost overwhelmed with attention. Now we can begin to understand—since here on earth we never get something for nothing—why it is that good wine cannot be sold cheaply, if it is true that time is money.

THE WINE INDUSTRY'S BY-PRODUCTS

The business of transforming grapes into wine leaves considerable residues, whose value depends to a great extent upon the ingenuity brought to their utilization, and it is worth remembering that nothing connected with the vine, nothing at all, need be wasted.

As we have seen, *eau-de-vie-de-marc* is made from the grapeskins, and the residue of that process, known as *murk*, forms a rich and valuable manure. The vine's foliage can be used as fodder for cattle, and the vine's stems, when it is past bearing, make excellent firewood, burning slowly and giving out tremendous heat. As for the grape pips, they form the most valuable by-product of all: the oil extracted from them is used in soap-making, and no doubt future research will discover many surprising uses for them. Indeed the treasures hidden in the residues of wine-making are still insufficiently exploited, and we are no longer rich enough to overlook any possibility.

CHAPTER 6

Wine and Food

"TO EACH ACCORDING TO HIS NEEDS . . ."

We know, since Molière said so, that we must eat to live and not live to eat, but the question whether we should drink with food or between meals is still an open one, and it is vain to try to lay down rigid rules for people who have both different tastes and different ways of life, and the functioning of whose digestive organs is infinitely varied.

The people of the Far East live on a handful of rice if they are poor, yet for all that the Chinese civilization has evolved a wonderful cuisine, deliciously described by Professor Huc. Madame David Neel lived in Tibet for many years and, like everyone else in that astonishing country, ate *tsampa,* which is barely-flour seasoned with butter and salt, and cooked slowly in a concoction of tea. The Indians of Canada, according to Grey Owl, that extraordinary "ambassador for the animals," live on fish and bannock, which is a sort of thick pancake made of rye or barley flour and cooked in the hot ashes of the campfire. Simply because the older cultures of Europe have developed a sophisticated cuisine, and because so many French people are born cooks, and because the art of eating well has, in recent years, been pretentiously dignified to the status of a pseudo-science—gastronomy—let us not assume that the French alone possess the ultimate truth concerning food preparation, and that the entire universe must guzzle to their tune on pain of instant excommunication.

Certainly it is pleasant to prepare wholesome dishes to assuage hunger, and the drinking of good wine in moderation and with discernment is something to be recommended—wine, intelligently chosen for our comfort and refreshment, and not only as an accompaniment to food—but it is intolerable to hear or read the solemn nonsense emanating from those imitation Brillat-Savarins who proliferated between the wars, delivering their inanities at the tops of their voices, or shedding them from their logorrhoeic pens. Soon the poor reader, bombarded by second-hand erudition and Dionysiac doggerel, no longer knows which way to turn, and nothing is more distressing—or more comic, if you like—than the seriousness with which these makeshift pontiffs pronounce upon the problems of gastronomy, formulating laws, imposing dogmas and sometimes, to cap it all, breaking the most elementary rules of grammar. God forbid that we should add a chapter to this mediocre literature. So we shall content ourselves with some reflections based on good sense, and aimed only at helping the reader decide for himself.

WHEN AND HOW TO DRINK WINE

Wine, whatever its quality or origin, should be taken neat and in small mouthfuls. Diluting it with water, with soda water even, was a heresy much committed in all innocence by the Americans fighting in France in 1918. The Italians have the right idea when they keep a large glass of fresh water at hand, and flank it with other glasses intended for wine.

Wine can be taken at any hour of the day, with meals, of course, and between meals no less. It is by no means wrong—indeed, it can even be recommended—to nibble tidbits while drinking wine, such as biscuits (either sweet or salt), walnuts, almonds, hazelnuts, even peanuts if you must, or scraps of one of the milder cheeses—Gruyère, for instance, or Port Salut, or a goat's-milk cheese. Morsels of this sort enhance a wine's qualities, especially when it is of rather lowly origin.

At table, if the repast has been sensibly arranged, it is the other way around—there the food is not expected to enhance the wine, for it is the duty of the wine to enhance the dishes with which it is served; but it is not enough simply to serve each dish with the wine that best suits it. From the start of the meal to its end, a skillful progression should be aimed at, and a light, delicate wine should precede a full-bodied one rather than follow it. Finally, avoid overdoing it—an interminable list of different vintages can only lead to confusion, so limit your choice to a few bottles of good origin that your guests will enjoy appraising at leisure.

As regards which wine goes with what food, the general rules can be easily summarized and, if no one's taste but your own was to be consulted, it would be simple to remark that preference should take precedence over rules, and that the right wine to drink with any particular dish is the one you prefer to drink with it. Indeed there is no strict etiquette in the matter, but your guests have to be considered, and long experience has taught us that most people's likes and dislikes incline to over-all agreement.

For instance, hardly anyone would care to drink red wine with fish, and many people would be ill if they attempted it. A dry white wine is what goes well with fish—Chablis with oysters, for instance, and Montrachet with grilled or poached sole. If the fish is served in sauce, the wine need not be quite so dry, and you can serve a Pouilly-Fuissé, for instance, or a white Alsatian, or, since our remarks concerning red wine do not apply to pink, a good *rosé* such as Tavel. In fact, *rosé* goes well with all food except dessert, and it is especially good with white meats such as veal and lamb, and with roast chicken, partridge or pheasant; but it should be borne in mind that only Tavel travels well. The lighter Anjou, and still lighter Coulins, are not to be trusted very far afield.

The darker the meat the darker the wine, and Chambertin, traditionally the wine to serve with roast duck, also goes particularly well with roast beef, roast venison and jugged hare, while Châteauneuf-du-Pape is a superb accompaniment to grilled steak in all its forms. In any case, it is usual to serve red wine, either Burgundy or Claret, with meat dishes, but while most people agree that this is the best arrangement, no harm will come from drinking white wine with meat. Sweet wines, of course, do not go with fish or meat, and the proper time to fill your guests' glasses with Sauternes or Barsac is when the fruit and nuts arrive, always remembering that Château-d'Yquem is the greatest dessert wine of all. Incidentally, sweet food kills the flavor of a dry wine stone dead, and no wine can stand up to highly spiced foods, except, perhaps, a Patrimoniaux from Corsica.

SERVING WINE

Choosing which bottles to offer to the appraisal of your guests requires mature reflection as you stand there in the cellar's cool silence. Presenting the wines correctly, producing them at the desired moment, these things involve delicate problems that you must solve with elegance and without apparent effort.

Wine is a living thing, and it must not be handled carelessly. Red wines cast a sediment, and this must not be disturbed as the bottles are carried from the cellar to the dining room. Remove the foil wrapping carefully, and wipe the cork and the top of the bottle before applying the corkscrew. For preference, use a corkscrew with levers of a tubular screw, but if you use an old-fashioned bottle-screw, be sure that its spiral is broad and flat, and before drawing the cork, wrap the bottle in a folded napkin; perhaps not one wine bottle in ten thousand is faulty, but if you happened to get that bottle and it broke as you struggled to draw its cork the consequences could be most unpleasant. So wrap the bottle's neck in a cloth, and draw the cork slowly and steadily, without agitating the wine. Incidentally, a cork can be removed without using a cork-screw at all—by thudding the bottom of the bottle against a soft vertical surface—but it's a method no wine-lover would use even if he found himself on a desert island with a bottle of wine and no corkscrew.

As regards red wine, put the bottles in the room where the wine is to be drunk so that it takes on the temperature of the room, and draw the corks at least an hour beforehand. This allows the wine to "breathe," and the cheaper the wine the longer it should be given. The action of the air mellows the wine, bringing out its flavor and its bouquet, and this is another reason why we recommend large glasses that need to be no more than half filled. However, if you decant the wine there is no need to allow it to breathe. And now we must make our choice between two methods of serving wine, irreconcilably opposed: is it better to serve the wine from its original bottle, lying indolently in a wickerwork cradle, wearing its label and a venerable coating of dust, or to decant it by pouring it with the minutest care, slowly and ungurglingly, into a glorious crystal decanter, regardlessly abandoning the bottle and consigning it to the lower depths?

Purists disapprove of bringing dusty bottles to the table, and there are some who think the use of the cradle pretentious, but others—and I am of their number—cherish a tender regard for the bottle in which the wine has slowly perfected itself; before they drink it, they want to dream a little as they contemplate, with a lively curiosity, the vessel that is about to yield its secret. In matters of this sort it is impossible to settle the argument, since each side is firmly entrenched in its own position and will remain so.

Now the time has come to taste the wine, so let us beat about the bush no longer, but actually drink some wine, an operation that will fortunately lead to no hair-splitting arguments.

TASTING THE WINE

To appreciate a wine's qualities calls for a great deal of care and attention, the seriousness appropriate to the performance of a rite, a profound knowledge of matters pertaining to the grapevine, and, if you charitably wish to communicate your sensations to others, the possession of a special vocabulary, which is, anyway, impoverished enough at that. To say of a wine that it is substantial, distinguished, harmonious, authoritative or complete represents but poorly the total effect of an assembly of olfactory and gustatory sensations that are easily perceived by the conscientious wine-taster, even if they are decidedly untranslatable. The man who wields the pen and wants to describe the taste of wine is faced with a task even more hopeless than that of describing a landscape or a pretty woman, and the best thing he can do is abandon the attempt as beyond human power.

At least let us lead from strength by not neglecting the elementary precautions intended to secure the most favorable conditions for judging wine expertly. "The first thing to do when tasting," writes Paul de Cassagnac, "is to inhale deeply, which enables the bouquet to be appreciated."

This is the other reason for only half-filling the glass —so that a gyratory movement can be imparted to the liquid, encouraging the wine's aroma to rise. Next the taster lifts the glass to his lips and lets a mouthful of the wine flow over his tongue. Paul de Cassagnac continues: "The taster makes the wine pass over that part of his tongue where the taste buds are particularly sensitive, then he raises it toward his palate in order to get a clear impression of its fragrance. Next he swallows half of it, and at the same moment slightly opens his lips, a difficult knack to acquire and one that often causes amusing mishaps among beginners. Then he inhales a light breath of air, which becomes charged with the wine's aroma and caresses the palate. Finally, the mouth is closed, and the taster goes through the motions of chewing the wine."

Of course, as we've already remarked, the wine must be served at its appropriate temperature, but as regards this serious matter there is some division of opinion. So, for what it is worth, we will state our personal view. Everyone knows that white wine must be chilled, and red wine served at room temperature, but is it possible to be more precise than this? Red wine reveals its quality at a temperature of about 20° C. if full-bodied, and at 16° C. if less substantial, while very light red wine and *rosé* wines such as Bourgueil and Tavel gain from being served cooler still. Dry white wine should be served at about 10° C. to

12° C., which is the recommended cellar temperature, while the mellow white wines of Bordeaux, Monbazillac and Anjou should be served very cold, that is to say, at between 5° C. and 10° C. On the other hand, I remain implacably hostile to the practice of placing the bottles of wine in a refrigerating mixture of ice and rock salt, an operation that, in my opinion, is injurious to the wine and seriously disturbing to sensitive palates. Only sparkling wines may be subjected to this rough treatment, which slows down the rising of the tiny bubbles in a way that is pleasant to watch if the wine is being served in a tall glass; for this reason that shape is to be preferred to the shallow cup-shaped glass. Above all, in drinking champagne, never commit the unpardonable sin of agitating the wine with one of those absurd swizzle-sticks seen in night clubs and on the tables of ignorant vulgarians. If the effervescence bothers you, drink a *crémant** or, better, a still champagne, but don't destroy, with your sacrilegious swizzle-sticks—you, especially, mesdames—the patient endeavors of the champagne-grower. A sparkling wine of quality is not lemonade.

By the way, it is customary for you as host to pour a little wine into your own glass and drink it before serving your guests. The idea of this may once have been to show that the wine wasn't poisoned, but nowadays it

*Wine whose effervescence is imprisoned in the bottle at a pressure of 2 to 3 atmospheres, instead of 6 atmospheres, which is the normal pressure for champagne. A word of warning, however—don't confuse *crémant*, which is a kind of champagne, with *Cramant*, which is a *cru*.

is done simply to get rid of any scraps of floating cork, and to discover if the wine is sound. Occasionally, bacteria are entrapped in a bottle and give the wine a musty flavor, and sometimes a cork rots, contaminating the wine, which is then said to be "corked." A cork should smell of the wine when you draw it, and if it has the smell of cork there's usually something wrong. A corked wine is useless. You can neither drink it nor cook with it, but your wine-merchant will exchange it, and so will the wine-waiter in any restaurant of standing.

WINE IN THE KITCHEN

Wine's balanced composition, in which many ingredients that still defy analysis play a part, explains and justifies the traditional popularity in France of what Pasteur called "the healthiest and most hygenic of drinks." While the winegrowers, guided by the scientists, strive tirelessly to perfect the culture of the vine and the technique of wine-making, their customers also perform miracles, notably in those unpretentious laboratories that are our kitchens; it is especially in France's classic cuisine that wine and *eau-de-vie* have triumphed, forming as they do the essential basis for a prodigious variety of subtle sauces, appetizing marinades and savory entremets.

The use of wine in cookery must be almost as old as civilization. The Greeks and the Israelites both cooked with wine, and so did the Romans, as we know from recipes that have come down to us in Apicius's *De Re Coquinaria,* and it is clear that mankind long ago discovered that three attributes of food are improved by wine—its texture, its flavor and its nutriment. No doubt much of the meat of classical and biblical times was tough, and would have been almost inedible without prolonged marinading and slow cooking in wine. But no people have done more than the French toward raising the practice to the dignity of an art.

We have not the space to go deeply into the subject, or to include more than three or four traditional recipes, but we should be failing in our task if we did less; how could we bring out a book on French wines without at least mentioning Coq au Vin, Boeuf à la Bourguignonne and one or two other famous dishes?

Let us start with a celebrated fish dish—Moules à la Marinière. There will be enough for four persons if we take:

4 qts. mussels	2 glasses of dry white wine (preferably Bordeaux)
2 medium onions	2 ozs. butter
2 or 3 shallots	1 tbsp. parsley, finely chopped
2 cloves garlic	Juice of 1 lemon
A bouquet of parsley, thyme and bay	Pepper

Salt

Clean the mussels well in running water, throwing out any that are already open. Chop up the onions, shallots and garlic, and put them, with the mussels, in a large saucepan, adding the bouquet, salt, pepper, butter and about half the wine. Cover the pan and cook briskly over a good fire, shaking the pan, until all the mussels are open, which will take four of five minutes. Take the mussels out and remove the upper shells. Pour the liquor with the chopped vegetables into a bowl, and while the sediment is settling, put the mussels back into the saucepan in their half-shells, covering it to keep them warm.

Put the chopped vegetables into another pan with the rest of the wine, simmer and reduce a little, then pour in the liquor that the mussels were cooked in. Let this reduce by nearly a half, then season, adding the lemon juice and chopped parsley. Put the mussels into a shallow dish, pour the sauce over them, and serve.

Coq au Vin is a popular dish throughout France, and there are almost as many recipes for it as there are *départements,* but they all agree in requiring a chicken and a bottle of red wine:

1 3-lb. dressed chicken	1 glass of cognac
25 small onions	Lemon juice
1/2 lb. mushrooms	Pepper
2 cloves garlic	Salt
5 ozs. butter	1 bottle red wine

Put the butter into a deep, lidded pan and brown the chicken in it after seasoning the bird inside and out with lemon juice, salt and pepper. Now pour the brandy over the bird, putting a match to it, and as soon as the flames have died, pour on all the red wine—Châteauneuf-du-Pape is excellent for the purpose, or a medium Burgundy such as Nuits-Saint-Georges. Put the bird's giblets into the pan and simmer it, covered, for anything up to four hours—this is best done on the top of the stove and as slowly as possible.

Brown the onions in butter, and glaze them with sugar and a little red wine. Then sauté the mushrooms. When the chicken is tender, remove the giblets from the pan and put in the mushrooms, onions and crushed garlic.

Carve the chicken on a hot dish and pour the sauce over the pieces with the mushrooms and onions on top.

It was the chefs of Burgundy who invented Coq au Vin, one of a score of dishes for which the region is renowned, and now let us meet the most famous of all:

Boeuf à la Bourguignonne

2 lbs. stewing steak, cut in thickish slices
4 onions
1/2 lb. carrots
6 ozs. mushrooms
2 shallots
2 cloves garlic
2 rashers of bacon
1/2 bottle of a good red Burgundy
1 glass cognac
2 dsps. cooking oil

Chop fine the onions, mushrooms, garlic, shallots and carrots. Put one of the bacon rashers in the bottom of a saucepan and pour the oil over it. Then add all the chopped carrots. On them place a layer of beef, then salt and pepper. Next put in a layer of all the other chopped vegetables, well mixed. Follow it with a second layer of beef, then salt and pepper again before adding a second layer of chopped vegetables. Finally, put on another layer of beef and cover it with the other rasher of bacon. Pour in the wine and the cognac, then, for the third time, salt and pepper. Put the saucepan on the stove and cover it as soon as it starts to boil. Then leave it to simmer for six hours over the lowest possible flame.

Cheese and wine complement each other to perfection, and nothing can confirm this statement better than the following:

Fondue de Franche Conte

½ lb. Gruyère cheese, grated
6 eggs
1 gill of dry white wine
2 ozs. butter
1 clove garlic
Black pepper, freshly ground
Salt

Chop up the garlic and put it into a saucepan with the wine, then simer until the wine is reduced by half. Strain out the garlic and leave the wine to cool.

Beat up the eggs, cheese, butter, pepper and salt in a bowl, then stir in the wine, and put the mixture into a fireproof dish. Cook very gently over a low flame until a creamy mass forms, whereupon you serve at once while the fondue is piping hot. Your guests should be supplied with little strips of toast that can be dipped into the fondue either with the fingers or by the help of a fork.

On that note we must leave the subject of "food and wine," for we haven't the leisure to venture further into the enchanted province of culinary preparations, so let us end the chapter by repeating Brillat-Savarin's shrewd observation: "Food without wine is like a day without sunshine."

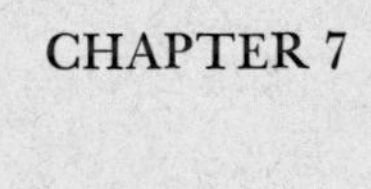

CHAPTER 7

The Wine Cellar and Its Treasure

THE CELLAR ITSELF

The reasons for storing wine in cellars rather than in attics or anywhere else are manifold—wine likes a cool and constant temperature (12° C. is considered ideal), the corks like a humid atmosphere and light is wine's worst enemy, after a fluctuating temperature. Moreover, wine dislikes vibration, and no room in the house is as still as its cellar.

Unfortunately, in these days of restricted accomodation, not everyone has a cellar, and since this chapter is intended primarily for the beginner who plans to lay down wine, we would suggest that, lacking a cellar, he adapt a large cupboard, one as remote from his living quarters as possible, and nowhere near any hot pipes. Cupboards under stairs make good wine-stores, and it is surprising how much wine can be kept in a small area.

All bottles of wine, except fortified wine, should be stored lying on their sides—to keep the corks moist—and so the cellar or cupboard must be fitted with shelves or, better still, with bins, and the most satisfactory bins are lozenge-shaped so that, when one bottle is removed, the others can't roll about. If the atmosphere is excessively dry, drape a damp cloth over the bins, and remember to keep it moist, and keep a thermometer near the wine. You have no cause to worry if the prevailing temperature of your wine store is as high as 15° C. or as low as 9° C., but if you find it fluctuating wildly between these two extremes you should discover the reason for it and remedy it.

Although we normally store other objects, such as books, with the heaviest at the bottom and the lightest on top, with wine it's the other way round. So store your white wine nearest the floor where it's cool, with your *vin rosé* immediately above it, your clarets and lighter red Burgundies, such as Beaujolais and Macon, next, and the other Burgundies on top. All wine should be allowed several days in the cellar before serving to acclimatize itself, and the more sediment a wine has, the more necessary this is. Most wine-lovers find pleasure in keeping a cellar-book and, in any case, it is of great practical value—it enables you to repeat your successes and to avoid repeating your mistakes. A simple exercise book with waterproof covers is all that is required, and we suggest that you rule its pages into five columns headed *Date*; *Wine*; *Amount bought*; *Merchant*; *Remarks*.

BUYING WINE

"I wonder often what the Vintners buy
One half so precious as the stuff they sell."
Rubáiyát of Omar Khayyam

That was just one of the many things that puzzled old Omar, and perhaps the lines explain how it is that only a minority of wine-merchants can be trusted to give really reliable advice regarding their stock in trade.

In fact, not so long ago, a wine-merchant was heard to remark: "I've still got a bottle of the 1877 Château Lafite downstairs, but I won't sell it, not the last bottle."

The truth is that for the connoisseur as well as for the beginner a good wine-merchant is almost "as precious as the stuff he sells," and it is sad to reflect that in Paris today, as well as in London and New York, there are men selling wine who know little more about it than slot-machines know about cigarettes. So if you do manage to find a knowledgeable and helpful wine-merchant, fasten to him like a limpet; no one will blame you if you keep his name a secret from your friends.

Before you buy a case of an untried wine, buy a bottle; better still, buy a half-bottle, and, if you like it, remember that a whole bottle can be reasonably expected to be even better. Great wine does not like being imprisoned in a small bottle, and it is usually at its best in a magnum. On the other hand, when buying *eau-de-vie,* the smaller the bottle the better. As soon as you open a bottle of cognac, evaporation begins, and a little of the spirit's quality is lost at each successive opening.

Much money can be saved by buying wine young and laying it down for a number of years, but if you're philistine enough to look upon wine as a speculative investment—as if wine were stocks and bonds—you're probably in for some disappointing experiences. Certainly we hear stories of private cellars appreciating enormously in value, but this is often due more to luck than to judgment, and as a general thing speculation in vintage wine isn't a field in which the amateur can compete with the professional. Besides, fashions in wine-drinking change, and who can say that the next generation won't revert to the ways of our eighteenth-century ancestors and kill the demand for mature wine by deciding that the product should be drunk quite young?

Where a knowledgeable wine-merchant can be of the greatest help is in the matter of the best vintages for a given wine. An elaborate and detailed vintage chart is not to be scorned as a rule-of-thumb guide, but those tiny charts printed in pocket diaries or distributed by wholesalers are often next to useless. I have two before me as I write. For 1956 one gives Burgundy a slightly better than average rating, while the rating of the other is slightly below average—and, in a sense, they both are right. As regards red Burgundy, 1956 was a poor year, but for white Burgundy it was well above average, and for some *crus* it was the best year of the decade. Indeed, there are too many subtleties and imponderables in wine production for generalization, and no chart can compete with the opinion of an experienced vintner, who spends his life tasting wine and purveying it.

If our remarks upon how to buy are a little sketchy, we can at least be more precise in the matter of what to buy. Our suggestions comprise only a small cellar, but one, we trust, that will form a sound foundation for bigger and better things.

A MODEST CELLAR

We will start with white wines, as they go nearest the floor, and work our way up. In Appendix IV to this volume we have reproduced a sumary vintage chart which will help to suggest appropriate vintage years.

White Burgundy

1/2 doz. bottles of Chablis.
1/2 doz. bottles of Pouilly-Fuissé.
1/2 doz. bottles of Montrachet.
1 doz. bottles of a cheaper white Burgundy, such as Les Combettes or Les Pucelles.

White Bordeaux

1 doz. bottles dry Graves, preferably Château-bottled.
1/2 doz. bottles Sauternes or Barsac, preferably Château-bottled.

Vins Rosés

1 doz. bottles of *rosé* wine from Tavel.

Clarets

1 doz. bottles of Saint-Emilion.
1/2 doz. bottles of Château-Haut-Brion.
1 doz. bottles of Château-Haut-Brion for keeping.

Red Burgundy

1 doz. bottles of a young Beaujolais.

1 doz. bottles of Nuits-Saint-Georges, preferably estate-bottled.

$^1/_2$ doz. bottles of Chambertin.

Rhône Wine

1 doz. bottles of Châteauneuf-du-Pape.

Champagne

$^1/_2$ doz. bottles of Dom Pérignon.

Eaux-de-vie

1 bottle of cognac.

1 bottle of armagnac.

Thus we come to the end of our monograph, and surely we can do no better than conclude with the words of Olivier de Serres, the father of French agriculture: "After bread came wine, the Creator's second gift for the sustenance of life, and first in order of excellence." (*Théâtre de l'Agriculture,* 1600.)

Appendixes

I. The Composition of Wine

Normal wine has two major constituents, water and ethyl alcohol, accompanied by a great number of minor constituents that, although quantitively small, nevertheless play an important part in the food value of wine. Note that the alcoholic content of wine obtained by normal fermentation does not exceed 17° in theory or 15° in practice, which means that wines having any higher alcoholic content—i.e. fortified wines—have to be reinforced by the addition of foreign alcohol.

Ethyl alcohol (C_2H_6O) is a volatile liquid that smells faintly and not disagreeably of ether. Since it is a carbohydrate, releasing heat and energy, it is a food, and there is nothing in its composition to suggest that it is in any way poisonous. It has a specific action upon the nervous system, inducing stimulation that finds both muscular and mental expression, and these functional changes are perfectly normal—and beneficial—if wine is taken in moderation, but, of course, become uncontrollable if moderation is eschewed.

As for the numerous constituents of wine other than water and ethyl alcohol, its vitamins merit special mention. As might be expected, wine carries the grapes' vitamins into the body: the antiscorbutic vitamin C and vitamin P. Lavollay and Sevestre attribute a good part of the tonic action of wine to its richness in vitamin P.

II. Viticultural Evolution Since 1790

Many people are under the impression that the crises that have harassed French viticulture during the present century—notably between 1904 and 1908, and between 1930 and 1935—are exceptional, but in fact they are only recurrences of comparable disasters met with in the course of past history.

The first reliable statistics, compiled in 1790, credit France, including the Rhine's left bank, with 1,674,489 hectares during the course of the next ten years. However, French consumption was far from able to absorb the national production, and Lavoisier estimated that only a little over 7,000,000 hectoliters of wine was consumed out of the 25,000,000 hectoliters produced annually. More precise evaluations were made between 1804 and 1808, to serve as a basis for reimposing the tax on wine, and by 1816 French consumption did not exceed 14,000,000 hectoliters. In 1827, 1,155,073 hectoliters were exported, and 5,229,880 hectoliters were distilled, leaving 28,000,000 hectoliters to be consumed, a great part of which was lost, since the French consumption of wine at that time was a long way from reaching one hectoliter per head. Overabundant harvests, notably those of 1818 and 1833, continued to engender a succession of crises, and the condition of the winegrowers remained desperate. In 1810 the naturalist Bosc wrote: "Of all crops, the grapevine is the least advantageous."

In 1848 the wines of the Midi were selling at 5 francs a hectoliter, and one of the first tasks of the Second

Republic was to find remedies for the slump in wine sales. The Legislative Assembly decided to conduct an inquest into the viticultural situation, but the catastrophic arrival of the oidium in 1852 brought about an unexpected end to the slump by reducing annual production to an average 15,000,000 hectoliters during the next five years. The discovery of a remedy for oidium—dusting the vines with flowers of sulphur—induced a return to overproduction from 1857 on. However, the growth of the railways in that period, and the increase in steam navigation, opened up new channels of export, and there was much planting of new stocks, remarkable for their high yield. In particular the Languedoc plain became a veritable sea of that highly productive vine, the Aramon, and in 1875 the zenith of French viticulture was reached: 2,500,000 hectares of vines provided 84,000,000 hectoliters of wine, which was disposed of without difficulty. An incredible prosperity spread throughout the winegrowing regions, but, unfortunately, it was not to last.

The commercial treaties of 1860 confronted the winegrowing regions of the south with uncertainties thitherto unknown, and at the same time a crisis overtook northern viticulture, which led to the disappearance of the vine from the area around Paris, as well as from the Oise, the Eure and the Eure-et-Loir—a retreat that was hastened by the invasions of the phylloxera and the mildew. From 1876 to 1893 these two plagues presented the whole of French viticulture with an enormous crisis, and it was estimated that the phylloxera alone destroyed nearly a million hectares of vines. However, good can come from evil, and one effect of these disasters was the realization that the fluctuation of the economic structure could only be combated by concerted action in the form of a professional organization. Today French viticulture is organized on a national scale through representative bodies of winegrowers in constant touch with I.N.A.O.—in full, the *Institut National des Appellations d'Origine des Vins et Eaux-de-Vie*—and the last fifty years have seen a steady improvement in standard and a rational curbing of overproduction.

III. Cooperage

Each of the winegrowing regions has its own method of cooperage, and for those who contemplate buying wine in cask we append these notes, giving the more important units.

Champagne. The standard barrel is the *queue,* containing 216 liters and yielding approximately 270 bottles. There is also a *demi-queue.*

Burgundy. The standard barrel is the *pièce,* containing an average of 227 liters and approximately 290 bottles.

2 *feuillettes*	=	1 *pièce*
2 *quartauts*	=	1 *feuillette*
57 liters	=	1 *quartaut*

The Beaujolais *pièce* contains 216 liters, and the Mâconnais *pièce* 215 liters. For Chablis, the standard barrel is the *feuillette* of 136 liters.

Bordeaux. The standard measure is the *tonneau,* but the barrel of that name is obsolete. A *tonneau* consists of four *barriques,* or 225 liters. Half a *barrique* is a *feuillette.*

Alsace. There is really no standard barrel, but it is quite usual for the wine to be sold by the enormous thousand-liter *foudre.*

Other Measures. The standard barrel for the whole of the Rhône Valley, and for Touraine, is the *pièce,* holding 225 liters. However, farther down the Loire the 220'liter *pièce* is standard.

The wines of the Midi are sold by the *hectoliter* (22 gallons).

IV. The Best Vintages of Recent Years in Suggested Order of Merit

Champagne. 1959; 1961; 1955; 1953; 1957.
Red Burgundy. 1959; 1955; 1961; 1953; 1957.
White Burgundy. 1959; 1955; 1961; 1957; 1953.
Red Bordeaux. 1959; 1961; 1955; 1957; 1953.
White Bordeaux. 1959; 1955; 1953; 1961; 1957.
Rhône. 1955; 1957; 1961; 1959.
Loire. 1959; 1961; 1957; 1955; 1953.
Alsace. 1959; 1961; 1955; 1952; 1953.

V. Summary of French Wines

CHAMPAGNE

The *appellation contrôlée* "Champagne" may be applied only to sparkling wines made in the ancient province of Champagne (the Marne, parts of the Aisne and Aube, with a few communes in the Haute-Marne and Seine-et-Marne) in the recognized way, and the only grapes currently admitted are the Pinot-Noir, Pinot Meunier, Chardonnay, Arbanne and Petit Meslier. Alone of *appellations contrôlées,* that of Champagne need not be printed on the bottle labels and, in fact, never is.

BURGUNDY

The viticultural area of Burgundy comprises the whole of the *départements* of the Yonne, Côte d'Or and Saône-et-Loire, with a small part of the *département* of the Rhône.

Appellations contrôlées applying to the whole area are "Bourgogne," "Bourgogne Rosé" and "Bourgogne Clairet." The alcoholic content of wines claiming these appellations must not be less than 10° for red wines or 10.5° for white, and very stringent conditions are laid down regarding the grapes such wines may be made from.

Only slightly inferior are the *appellations contrôlées* "Bourgogne Ordinaire," "Bourgogne Ordinaire Rosé" and "Bourgogne Aligote," and here the required minimum alcoholic content is 9° for the red wines and 9.5° for the white.

The rather rare *appellation contrôlée* "Bourgogne

Passe-Tous-Grains" is confined to red wines, and it demands a minimum alcoholic content of 9.5°.

LOWER BURGUNDY

The areas covered by the four Chablis appellations are in process of revision. All four apply to white wine produced in the Yonne, and they are:

Appellation contrôlée "Petit Chablis," requiring a minimum alcoholic content of 9.5°; *appellation contrôlée* "Chablis," requiring 10°; *appellation contrôlée* "Chablis Premier Cru," requiring 10.5°; and *appellation contrôlée* "Chablis Grand Cru," requiring a minimum of 11°. The *appellation contrôlée* "Rosé des Riceys" is confined to *rosé* wines grown in a small area south of Troyes, and as production is extremely low the wine is unlikely to be encountered except by visitors to the district.

UPPER BURGUNDY

The winegrowing areas of the Côte d'Or, though of great viticultural importance, are of small extent and comprise only the adjacent Côte de Nuits and Côte de Beaune districts.

Côte de Nuits. Grands Crus with *appellations contrôlées*: Chambertin, Chambertin-Cos de Bèze, Ruchottes-Chambertin, Latricières-Chambertin, Mazis-Chambertin, Griottes-Chambertin, Chapelle-Chambertin, Charmes-Chambertin; Clos de la Roche; Clos Saint-Denis; Bonnes Mares; Clos de Tart; Clos de Vougeot; Musigny; Echézeaux, Grands Echézeaux; Romanée-Conti, Romanée-Saint-Vivant, Richebourg, La Tache.

Wines not entitled to the above appellations, but produced within the delimited area of their respective communes, are entitled to the following seven *appellations contrôlées*: Fixin, Gevrey-Chambertin, Chambolle-Musigny, Vosne-Romanée, Morey-Saint-Denis, Vougeot, Nuits-Saint-Georges.

Côte de Beaune. Grands Crus with *appellations contrôlées*: Corton, Corton-Charlemagne, Charlemagne; Montrachet, Chevalier-Montrachet, Bâtard-Montrachet, Criots-Bâtard-Montrachet, Bienvenues-Bâtard-Montrachet.

Wines not entitled to the above appellations, but produced within the delimited area of their respective communes, are entitled to the following twenty *appellations contrôlées*: Pommard, Volnay, Aloxe-Corton, Beaune, Pernand-Vergelesses, Monthélie, Blagny, Ladoix, Auxey-Duresses, Meursault, Saint-Aubin, Puligny-Montrachet, Chassagne-Montrachet, Santenay, Decize-les-Maranges, Sampigny-les-Maranges, Cheilly-les-Maranges, Chorey-les-Beaune, Savigny, Saint-Romain.

All other communes of the Côte de Beaune are covered by the *appellations contrôlées* "Côte-de-Beaune" and "Côte-de-Beaune-Villages."

With a few exceptions the required alcoholic content of the *Grands Crus* of both districts is 11.5° for the red wines and 12° for the white. As regards the other *crus* the figures are 10.5° and 11° respectively.

The Côte Chalonnaise. Red and white wines grown in the delimited areas of the communes of Mercurey, Saint-Martin-sous-Montaigu and Bourgneuf-Val-d'Or are entitled to the *appellation contrôlée* "Mercurey"; red and white wines grown in the Givry and Rully communes are entitled to *appellation contrôlée* "Givry" and *appellation contrôlée* "Rully" respectively; and white wines grown in the Montagny, Buxy, Saint-Vallerin and Jully-les-Buxy communes are entitled to the *appellation contrôlée* "Montagny."

The required alcoholic minimum for all the above *crus* is 10.5° for the red wines and 11° for the white.

THE MÂCONNAIS

The most important of Mâcon's appellations is the *appellation contrôlée* "Pouilly-Fuissé," confined to white wines grown in the Solutré-Pouilly, Fuissé, Chaintré and Vergisson communes from Pinot blanc and Chardonnay vines. Where a vineyard's name is coupled with that of "Pouilly-Fuissé," the required alcoholic minimum is 12°, otherwise 11°.

The district's other *appellations contrôlées* are "Pinot-Chardonnay-Mâcon," "Mâcon Superieur," "Mâcon Rouge," "Mâcon Rosé" and "Mâcon Blanc." The first two appellations require a minimum alcoholic content of 10° for the red wines and 11° for the white, and the other three require 9°whether red, *rosé* or white. Under certain conditions, thirty-nine communes are permitted to add their names to the "Mâcon" *appellation contrôlée.*

The *appellations contrôlées* "Pouilly-Vinzelles" and "Pouilly-Loché" refer to white wines grown in the named communes under the same conditions as those required for Pouilly-Fuissé.

THE BEAUJOLAIS

The "Crus de Beaujolais"—red wines only—are entitled to the following *appellations contrôlées*:

"Côte de Brouilly" and "Brouilly" for area within the Odenas, Saint-Lager, Cercié, Quincié and Charentay communes.

"Chénas" for areas of the Chénas and La Chapelle-de-Guinchay communes.

"Chiroubles" for areas within the commune of that name.

"Fleurie" for areas within the commune of that name.

"Juliénas" for areas of the Juliénas, Jullié, Emeringes and Pruzilly comunes.

"Morgon" for areas within the Villié-Morgon commune.

"Moulin-à-Vent" for areas within the Chénas and Romanèche-Thorins communes.

"Saint-Amour" for areas within the Saint-Amour-Bellevue commune.

Except for "Côte de Brouilly," which requires a minimum alcoholic content of 10.5°, all the above *crus* require 10°; and 11° is required when the vineyard's name is included in the appellation.

The area's other *appellations contrôlées are* "Beaujolais," "Beaujolais Supérieur" and "Beaujolais-Villages," the first requiring an alcoholic content of 9° and the other two ones of 10°. The appellations "Beaujolais" and "Beaujolais Supérieur" can refer to white wine, with a minimum alcoholic content of 9.5° and 10.5° respectively.

Under certain conditions thirty-five communes are permitted to join their names to that of Beaujolais in relation to red wines with a minimum alcoholic content of 10°

BORDEAUX

The viticultural area of Bordeaux comprises almost the whole of the Gironde *département,* and even the conditions required for the comprehensive regional *appellations contrôlées* "Bordeaux" and "Bordeaux Supérieur" are fairly stringent. These appellations apply both to red and white wines, "Bordeaux" requiring 9.75° of alcohol for the red wine and 10° for the white; and "Bordeaux Supérieur" requiring 10.5° and 11.5° respectively.

THE MÉDOC

The *appellation contrôlée* "Graves" and "Graves red wines, and a minimum alcoholic content of 10° is required. Superior to the "Médoc" appellation are the five *appellations contrôlées* of its five subdivisions: Haut-Médoc, Moulis, Pauillac, Saint-Estèphe and Saint-Julien. The last four appellations are superior to the first.

THE GRAVES

The *appellation contrôlée* "Graves" and "Graves Supérieur" are confined to red and white wines grown in forty-two named communes. The "Graves" appellation requires an alcoholic minimum of 10° and the "Graves Supérieur" appellation requires 12°; this is virtually the only difference.

The rather better *appellation contrôlée* "Cérons" is

confined to white wines grown in delimited areas of the Cérons, Podensac and Illats communes. An alcoholic minimum of 12.5° degrees is required.

SAUTERNES

The lordly *appellation contrôlée* "Sauternes" is confined to white wine grown in the Sauternes, Bommes, Fargues, Preignac and Barsac communes. The appellation's required contitions are most exacting, as is to be expected for Bordeaux's highest appellation, and a minimum alcoholic content of 13° is demanded.

Differences in the nature of the subsoil justify a separate *appellation contrôlée*—"Barsac"—but the conditions for the wine's production differ very little from those for Sauternes.

ENTRE-DEUX-MERS

Most of the white wine made in this productive area is entitled to no *appellation contrôlée* other than "Entre-deux-mers," and most of the red wine, even less favored, has to be content with the "Bordeaux" appellation; but the following six appellations are in a different class altogether:

Appellation contrôlée "Sainte-Croix-du-Mont," confined to white wines with an alcoholic minimum of 13° and produced under the same conditions as Sauternes.

Appellation contrôlée "Loupiac" confined to white wine produced in the Loupiac commune under conditions identical to those of the above.

Appellation contrôlée "Côtes de Bordeaux-Saint-

Macaire" is confined to white wines grown in ten named communes, with a required alcoholic minimum of 11°.

Appellation contrôlée "Premières Côtes de Bordeaux" is confined to red and white wines grown in thirty-seven named communes, and the required alcoholic minimum is 10.5°.

Appellation contrôlée "Sainte-Foy-Bordeaux" is confined to red and white wines grown in the delimited areas of the Sainte-Foy, Gensac, Pessac-sur-Dordogne, Landerraouat, Pellegrue and Massugas communes, and the required minimum of alcohol is 10.5° for the red wines and 11° for the white.

Appellation contrôlée "Graves de Vayres" is confined to red and white wines grown on gravel in the Vayres and Arvayres communes, and the required alcoholic minimum is 10.5° for the red wine and 11° for the white.

RIGHT BANKS OF THE DORDOGNE AND GIRONDE

Appellations contrôlées "Bourg," "Côtes de Bourg" and "Bourgeais" are confined to red and white wines from the Canton of Bourg, with a required alcoholic minimum of 10.5°.

Appellation contrôlée "Blaye" or "Blayais" is confined to red and white wines grown within the Blaye, Saint-Savin-de-Blaye and Saint-Ciers-sur-Gironde Cantons, and a minimum alcoholic content of 9.75° is required for the red wines and 10° for the white.

Appellation contrôlée "Premières Côtes de Blaye" is also confined to red and white wines grown in the Blaye, Saint-Savin-de-Blaye and Saint-Ciers-sur-Gironde Cantons, but the conditions are somewhat different, and the required alcoholic content is 10.5°.

Appellation contrôlée "Côtes de Blaye" is confined to white wines grown under conditions identical with those required for "Premières Côtes de Blaye," except as regards the varieties of grape used.

Appellation contrôlée "Côtes de Canon-Fronsac" is confined to red wines from a part of the communes of Fronsac and Saint-Michel-de-Fronsac, the *crus* being mainly Château Gazin, Grand Renouil, Pavillon and Toumalin. The required alcoholic minimum is 10.5°.

Appellation contrôlée "Côtes de Fronsac" relates to all red wines from Fronsac and Saint-Michel-de-Fronsac not covered by the above, as well as red wines from areas of the Saint-Aignan, La Rivière, Saillans and Galgon communes, the *crus* entitled to it being mainly the Châteaux Balloy, Chadenne, La Fontaine, Jeandeman, Magondeau, Plain-Pont, de Trois Croix, Vieille Curé and Vrai-Canon-Bouché. The required alcoholic minimum is 10.5°.

SAINT-EMILION

The appellation contrôlée "Saint-Émilion" is confined to red wines grown in the following eight comunes: Saint-Émilion, Saint-Christophe-des-Bardes, Saint-Laurent-des-Combes, Saint-Hippolyte, Saint-Etienne-de-Lisse, Saint-Pey-d'Armens, Vignonet and Saint-Sulpice-de-Faleyrans. The required alcoholic minimum is 10.5°.

A few years ago a definitive classification of the more important Saint-Émilion *crus* was authorized by I.N.A.O., from whom the full list can be obtained on request. Since it varies to some extent from year to year, it would not be practical to give it here.

The *appellations contrôlées* "Lussac-Saint-Émilion," "Montagne-Saint-Émilion," "Parsac-Saint-Émilion," "Puisseguin-Saint-Émilion" and "Saint-Georges-Saint-Émilion" are confined to red wines grown within the communes named in the appellations, and produced under the same conditions as "Saint-Émilion"; and the same conditions apply to the *appellation contrôlée* "Sables-Saint-Émilion," which is confined to an area of the Libourne commune, with a gravel subsoil.

POMEROL

The *appellation contrôlée* "Pomerol" is confined to red wines grown in the Pomerol commune, and a small part of the Libourne commune, produced under conditions differing only slightly from those of "Saint-Émilion." The same conditions apply to the *appellations contrôlées* "Lalande-de-Pomerol" and "Neac," which are confined to red wines grown within the communes named in the appellations.

THE LOIRE

THE NIVERNAIS AND BERRY

Appellations contrôlées. "Pouilly-sur-Loire" (white wines with 9° min.alc. content).

"Pouilly-Fumé" or "Blanc-Fumé-de-Pouilly" (white wines with 11° min. alc. content).

"Sancerre" (red, *rosé* and white wines with 10° min. alc. content for the red and *rosé*, 10.5° forth e white).

"Menetou-Salon" (red, *rosé* and white wines with 10° min. alc. content for the red and *rosé,* 10.5° for the white).

"Quincy" (white wines with 10.5° min. alc. content).

"Reuilly" (white wines with 10.5° min. alc. content).

TOURAINE

Appellations Contrôlées. "Touraine." This is the regional appellation for red, *rosé* and white wines grown under decreed conditions, and is inferior to the appellations listed below (9° min. alc. content for red and *rosé* wines, 9.5° for white).

"Bourgueil" and "Saint-Nicolas-de-Bourgueil" (red and *rosé* wines, with 9.5° min. alc. content).

"Chinon" (red and *rosé* wines, with 9.5° min. alc. content). A white "Chinon" wine is also produced, but in very small quantities.

"Vouvray" (white wines with 11° min. alc. content).

"Montlouis" (white wines with 10.5° min. alc. content).

Under certain conditions the word "*Pétillant*" may be used by the classified white wines of Touraine, Montlouis and Vouvray that have undergone a second fermentation in bottle.

"Touraine-Amboise" (red, *rosé* and white wines, with 9.5° min. alc. content for the red, 10° for the *rosé,* and 10.5° for the white).

"Touraine-Mesland" (red, *rosé* and white wines, with 10° min. alc. content for the red, and 10.5° for the *rosé* and white).

"Touraine-Azay-de-Rideau" (*white wines with 10° min. alc. content*).

"Touraine Mousseux" (sparkling red and white wines, produced by the Champagne process under decreed conditions).

"Vouvray Mousseaux" and "Montlouis Mousseux" (sparkling white wines produced by the Champagne process under decreed conditions).

ANJOU

Appellations Contrôlées. "Anjou" (the regional appellation for red and white wines, with 10° min. alc. content for the red, and 9.5° for the white).

"Rosé d'Anjou" (the regional appellation for *rosé* wines with 9° min. alc. content).

"Saumur" (white wines, with 10° min. alc. content).

Under decreed conditions the description *"Pétillant"* may be applied to "Rosé d'Anjou," which has undergone a second fermentation in bottle, and also to "Saumur" and "Anjou" white wines.

"Saumur-Champigny" (red wines with 10°min. alc. content).

"Coteaux de la Loire" (white wines with 12° min. alc. content).

"Coteaux du Layon" (white wines with 12° min. alc. content).

"Coteaux de l'Aubance" (white wines with 11° min. alc. content).

"Bonnezeaux" (white wines with 13.5° min. alc. content).

"Quarts de Chaume" (white wines with 13° min. alc. content).

"Savennières" (white wines with 12.5° min. alc. content).

A number of separate appellations, permitted under decree to Anjou wines, are to some extent self-explanatory: "Anjou-Rosé-de-Cabernet" (11°), "Saumur-Rosé de Cabernet" (12°), "Coteaux de l'Aubance Rosé de Cabernet" (12°), "Coteaux du Layon Rosé de Cabernet" (12°), "Anjou Mousseax" (10.5°) and "Saumur Mousseux" (10.5°).

MAINE

Appellations Contrôlées. "Coteaux du Loir" (red, rosé and white wines, with 9.5° min. alc. content for the red and *rosé,* and 10° for the white wines).

"Jasnières" (white wines with 10° min. alc. content).

THE ESTUARY AND COASTAL REGION

Appellation Contrôlées. "Muscadet" (white wines with 9.5° min. alc. content).

"Muscadet des Coteaux de la Loire" (white wines with 10° min. alc. content).

"Muscadet de Sèvre-et-Maine" (white wines with 10° min. alc. content).

"Pineau des Charentes" (*a vin de liqueur* with 16.5° min. alc. content and 22° maximum).

THE RHONE

APPELLATIONS CONTRÔLÉES

"Côtes-du-Rhône." This is the regional appellation covering red, *rosé* and white wines grown under decreed conditions in 128 communes on both banks of the Rhône. Normally the wines have a required alcoholic content of 10.5°, but when the name of the *département* of origin is added to the appellation, the required alcoholic content is 9.5°. The following five communes are entitled to add their names to the appellation: Cairanne (*rosé* and white, 12°), Chusclan (*rosé*, 12°), Gigondas (red, *rosé* and white, 12.5°), Vacqueyras (red, *rosé* and white, 12.5°) and Laudun (red and *rosé*, 12.5°, and white 12°).

"Côte-Rôtie" (red wines with 10° min. alc. content).

"Condrieu" (white wines with 11° min. alc. content).

"Château-Grillet" (white wine with 11° min. alc. content).

"Hermitage" or "L'Hermitage" (red, white and straw wines, with 10° min. alc. content for the red and white, and 14° for the straw wines).

"Crozes-Hermitage" (red and white wines, with 10° min. alc. content).

"Saint-Joseph" (red and white wines, with 10° min. alc. content).

"Cornas" (red wines with 11° min. alc. content).

"Saint-Peray" (white wines with 10° min. alc. content).

"Châteauneuf-du-Pape" (red and white wines with 12.5° min. alc. content).

"Tavel" (*rosé* wines with 11° min. alc. content).

"Lirac" (red, *rosé* and white wines with 11.5° min. alc. content).

"Muscat de Beaumes-de-Venise" (sweet white wines with 15° min. alc. content).

"Rasteau" (naturally sweet wines with a minimum alcoholic content of 21.5°, of which added alcohol must not amount to more than 6.5°).

"Clairette de Die" (sparkling wines with 10.5° min. alc. content).

PROVENCE

APPELLATIONS CONTRÔLÉES

"Palette" (red, *rosé* and white wines with, respectively, 10.5°, 11° and 11.5° min. alc. content).

"Cassis" (red, *rosé* and white wines, with 10.5° min. alc. content for the red and *rosé,* and 11° for the white wine).

"Bandol" (red, *rosé* and white wines, with 11° min. alc. content).

"Bellet" (red, *rosé* and white wines, with 10,5° min alc. content for the red and *rosé,* and 11° for the white).

LANGUEDOC

APPELLATIONS CONTRÔLÉES

"Clairette de Bellegrade" (white wines with 11.5° min. alc. content).

"Muscat de Frontignan" (sweet white wines with 15° min. alc. content).

"Muscat de Lunel" (sweet muscat wines with 15° min. alc. content).

"Muscat de Saint-Jean-de-Minervois" (sweet muscat wines, with 15° min. alc. content).

"Clairette du Languedoc" (Madeira-like wines, with 13° min. alc. content).

"Blanquette de Limoux," "Vin de Blanquette" and "Limoux Nature" (white wines, some sparkling, with 10° min. alc. content).

"Fitou" (red wines with 12° min. alc. content).

GAILLAC AND LOWER LANGUEDOC

Appellations Contrôlées. "Gaillac" (white wines with 10.5° min. alc. content).

"Gaillac Mousseux" (sparkling white wines with 10.5° min. alc. content).

"Gaillac Premières Côtes" (white wines with 12° min. alc. content).

ROUSSILLON

APPELLATIONS CONTRÔLÉES

"Grand Roussillon." This is the regional appellation for *vins doux naturels* and *vins de liqueur* made from red, *rosé* and white wines, and requiring a minimum alcoholic strength of 15°.

"Banyuls" (*vins doux naturels* and *vins de liqueur* made from red, *rosé* and white wines, with 15° min. alc. content). This is generally held to be the region's best appellation, others that cover similar wines with the same alcoholic content being "Maury," "Côtes d'Agly," "Côtes de Haut-Roussillon" and "Rivesaltes."

BÉARN AND BIGORRE

APPELLATIONS CONTRÔLÉES

"Jurançon" (white wines with 11° min. alc. content).

"Madiran" (red wines with 11° min. alc. content).

"Pacherenc du Vic-Bilh" (white wines with 12° min. alc. content).

PERIGORD AND QUERCY

APPELLATIONS CONTRÔLÉES

"Bergerac" (red and white wines, with, respectively, 10° and 11° min. alc. content).

"Bergerac Supérieur" (red and white wines with, respectively, 11° and 12° min. alc. content).

"Montbazillac" (sweet white wines with 13° min. alc. content).

"Montravel" (white wines with 12.5° min. alc. content).

"Haut-Montravel" (white wines with 12° min. alc. content).

"Côtes de Montravel" (white wines with 12° min. alc. content).

"Rosette" (white wines with 12° min. alc. content).

"Pécharmant" (red wines with 11° min. alc. content).

"Côtes de Duras" (red and white wines with, respectively, 10° and 10.5° min. alc. contents).

THE JURA

APPELLATIONS CONTRÔLÉES

"Côte du Jura." This is the regional appellation covering the *département*'s whole viticultural area for all types of wine produced: red, *rosé,* white, straw wines and *vins jaunes.* A minimum alcoholic content of 10° required for the red, *rosé* and white wines, 11° for the *vins jaunes,* and 18° for the straw wines (*vin de paille*).

"Arbois" (red, *rosé* and white wines and *vins jaunes,* with 10° min. alc. content for the red and *rosé* wines, 10.5° for the white wines, and 11.5° for the *vins jaunes*).

"Étoile" (white, *vin de paille, vin jaune,* with 10° min. alc. content for the red, and 10.5° for the white).

"Château-Chalon" *vins jaunes,* with 12° min. alc. content).

SAVOY AND BUGEY

APPELLATIONS CONTRÔLÉES

"Seyssel" (white wines, with 10° min. alc. content).

"Crepy" (white wines, with 9.5° min. alc. content).

ALSACE

There are no *appellations contrôlées* in Alsace, but for white wines to be entitled to the appellation "Vin d'Alsace" they must be made from Traminer, Riesling, Pinot or Muscat grapes, and the required minimum of alcoholic content is 8°. The words "Reserve Speciale," "Grand Vin," "Grand Reserve" or "Grand Cru" printed on the bottle labels indicate a superior wine with a required minimum alcoholic content of 10°.

Note: For reasons of space we have had to omit a number of wines that are not entitled to *appellation contrôlée,* but that are entitled to a lesser appellation to be seen on bottle labels in the form "*Appellation V.D.Q.S.,*" the initials standing for *Vins Delimités de Qualité Supérieure.* Full details of these *crus* can be obtained from I.N.A.O.

VI. The Official 1855 Classification of the Great Growths of the Gironde

In 1855 an official classification was made of the principal wines of the Bordeaux area. Despite certain inherent defects, some of which will be mentioned below, the 1855 classification remains today a remarkably accurate guide for the consumer.

1. CLARTES (MÉDOC AND GRAVES)

Growth	*Commune*
First Growth (Premiers Crus)	
Château Lafite-Rothschild	Pauillac
Château Margaux	Margaux
Château Latour	Pauillac
Château Haut-Brion	Pessac, Graves
Second Growths (Deuxièmes Crus)	
Château Mouton-Rothschild	Pauillac
Château Rausan-Ségla	Margaux
Château Rausan-Gassies	Margaux
Château Léoville-Las-Cases	Saint Julien
Château Léoville-Poyferré	Saint Julien
Château Léoville-Barton	Saint Julien
Château Durfort-Vivens	Margaux
Château Lascombes	Margaux
Château Gruaud-Larose	Saint Julien
Château Brane-Cantenac	Margaux-Cantenac
Château Pichon-Longueville	Pauillac
Château Pichon-Longueville-Comtesse de Lalande	Pauillac

Château Ducru-Beaucaillou	Saint Julien
Cos d'Estournel	Saint Estèphe
Château Montrose	Saint Estèphe
Third Growths (Troisièmes Crus)	
Château Giscours	Margaux-Labarde
Château Kirwan	Margaux-Cantenac
Château d'Issan	Margaux-Cantenac
Château Lagrange	Saint Julien
Château Langoa-Barton	Saint Julien
Château Malescot-Saint Exupéry	Margaux
Château Cantenac-Brown	Margaux-Cantenac
Château Palmer	Margaux-Cantenac
Château Grand La Lagune	Ludon
Château Desmirail	Margaux
Château Calon-Ségur	St. Estèphe
Château Ferrière	Margaux
Château Marquis d'Alesme-Becker	Margaux
Château Boyd-Cantenac	Margaux-Cantenac
Fourth Growths (Quatrièmes Crus)	
Château Saint Pierre-Bontemps	Saint Julien
Château Saint Pierre-Sevaistre	Saint Julien
Château Branaire-Ducru	Saint Julien
Château Talbot	Saint Julien
Château Duhart-Milon	Pauillac
Château Pouget	Margaux-Cantenac
Château La Tour-Carnet	Saint Laurent
Château Rochet	Saint Estèphe
Château Beychevelle	Saint Julien
Château Cantenac-Prieuré (now known as	Margaux-Cantenac

Prieuré-Lichine)	
Château Marquis-de-Terme	Margaux
Fifth Growths (Cinquièmes Crus)	
Château Pontet-Canet	Pauillac
Château Batailley	Pauillac
Château Grand-Puy-Lacoste	Pauillac
Château Grand-Puy-Ducasse	Pauillac
Château Lynch-Bages	Pauillac
Château Lynch-Moussas	Pauillac
Château Dauzac	Margaux-Labarde
Château Mouton d'Armailhacq	Pauillac
Château du Tertre	Margaux-Arsac
Château Haut-Bages-Libéral	Pauillac
Château Pédesclaux	Pauillac
Château Belgrave	Saint Laurent
Château Camensac	Saint Laurent
Château Cos Labory	Saint Estèphe
Château Clerc-Milon-Mondon	Pauillac
Château Calvé-Croizet-Bages	Pauillac
Château Cantemerle	Macau

2. SAUTERNES AND BARSAC

Growth	*Commune*
Grand First Growth (Premier Grand Cru)	
Château d'Yquem	Sauternes
First Growth (Premiers Crus)	
Château Giraud	Sauternes
Château La Tour Blanche	Bommes
Château Lafaurie-Peyraguey	Bommes
Château Rayne-Vigneau	Bommes

Château Rabaud-Promis	Bommes
Château Sigalas-Rabaud	Bommes
Château Haut-Peyraguey	Bommes
Château Coutet	Barsac
Château Climens	Barsac
Château de Suduiraut	Preignac
Château Rieussec	Farques
Second Growth (Deuxièmes Crus)	
Château Filhot	Sauternes
Château d'Arche	Sauternes
Château Lamothe	Sauternes
Château d'Arche-Lafaurie	Sauternes
Château Caillou	Barsac
Château Suau	Barsac
Château Nairac	Barsac
Château Doisy-Védrines	Barsac
Château Doisy-Daëne	Barsac
Château Doisy-Dubroca	Barsac
Château de Myrat	Barsac
Château Broustet	Barsac
Château de Malle	Preignac
Château Romer	Preignac

3. NOTES ON THE 1855 CLASSIFICATION

The Official Classification of Clarets recognized only wines from the Médoc region, with the single exception of the outstanding Graves, Château Haut-Brion. Many wine experts feel that other Graves, as well as some Pomerols and Saint-Émilions, deserve to be classed with the Médocs. Château Petrus from Pomerol, Château

Cheval-Blanc and Ausone from Saint-Émilion, and Château La Mission-Haut-Brion and Domaine de Chevalier from Graves are held by many to rank with the First Growth Médocs. Among the white wines, Châteaux Haut-Brion-Blanc, Carbonnieux and Olivier from the Graves region may be called comparable in rank to First Growth Sauternes and Barsac wines, although very different in character.

VII. Outstanding Burgundies

No official classification of the great Burgundies has been made, and, differences of opinion being wide and vehement, none is possible. The sequel is merely a summary of some of the most famous growths of Chablis and of the Côte d'Or, arranged by parish.

1. RED

Parish	*Growth*
Fixin	Les Arvelets
Fixy	Clos de la Perrière
Gevrey-Chambertin	Le Chambertin
	Clos de Bèze
	Le Latricières
	Clos St.-Jacques
	Les Variolles
Morey	Clos de Tart
	Clos des Lambrays
	Clos St.-Denis
Chambolle-Musigny	Le Musigny
	Les Bonnes Mares
	Les Amoureuses
Vougeot	Clos Vougeot
Flagey-Echezéaux	Les Grands-Echezéaux
	Echezéaux

Voane-Romanée	La Romanée-Conti La Tâche La Richebourg La Romanée-St.-Vivant
Nuits-Saint-Georges	Les Saint-Georges Les Vaucrains Les Porrets
Savigny-les-Beaune	Les Vergelesses
Beaune	Les Fèves Les Grèves Les Marconnets Les Clos des Mouches
Pommard	Les Rugiens Les Epenots Clos de la Commaraine
Volnay	Les Caillerets Les Fremiets Les Champans
Meursault	Santenots du Milieu
Chassange-Montrachet	Clos de la Boudriotte Clos Saint-Jean
Sautenay	Les Gravières
Pernaud	Ile des Vergelesses

2. WHITE

Parish	*Growth*
Puligny-Montrachet	Le Montrachet
	Le Chevalier-Montrachet
	Le Bâtard-Montrachet
	Les Combettes
Chassagne-Montrachet	Le Montrachet
	Le Bâtard-Montrachet
	Les Ruchottes
Meursault	Clos des Perrières
	Les Perrières
	Les Charmes
Aloxe-Corton	Corton-Charlemagne
Chambolle-Musigny	Le Musigny Blanc
Vougeot	Clos Blanc-de-Vougeot

3. CHABLIS (WHITE)

Blanchots
Bougros
Les Clos
Grenouilles
La Moutonne
Les Preuses
Valmur
Vaudésir

VIII. Capacity of Standard Bottles as Fixed by Decree

Champagne	80	centiliters
Burgundy	80	"
Bordeaux	75	"
Anjou	75	"
Alsace	72	"

Note: Wines entitled to the "Vin d'Alsace" appellation must be sold in the familiar slender bottle with a capacity of 72 centiliters. The bottles must be of green glass, in contradistinction to the hock bottle, which is red or brown.

IX. *Conversion Table: Degrees of Alcohol and Degrees of Proof Spirit*

Alcohol	*Proof Spirit*	*Alcohol*	*Proof Spirit*
1	1.8	9	15.9
2	3.7	10	17.7
3	5.6	11	19.4
4	7.2	12	21.2
5	8.9	13	23.1
6	10.7	14	24.7
7	12.4	15	26.4
8	14.2	16	28.1

Alcohol	*Proof Spirit*
17	29.9
18	31.6
19	33.4
20	35.2
22	37.0
21	38.9
23	40.7
24	42.6

Index

Allier, 52-53
Aloxe-Corton, 122
Alsace, 66, 79 ,137-38
Ancy, 66
Angelica, 79
Anisette, 80
Anjou, 54, 58-60, 131-32
Arbois, 137
Armagnac, 49, 76-77
Ars, 66
Auvergne, 52
Auxey-Duresses, 33, 122

Bandol, 26, 134
Banyuls, 25, 28, 135
Barsac, 126, 141-42
Bastia, 67
Bâtard-Montrachet, 122
Béarn 136
Beaujolais, 34-35, 124-25
Beaune, 32, 122
Bellet, 134
Benedictine, 78
Bergerac, 49, 50, 136
Berry, 53-55, 129-30
Bienvenus-Bâtard-Montrachet, 122
Bigorre, 136
Blagny, 122
Blanc-Fumé-de-Pouilly, 129
Blanquette de Limoux, 25, 27, 135
Blayais, 42, 48, 127
Blaye, 127
Blois, 56
Bonnes Mares, 121
Bonnezeaux, 131
Bordeaux, 40-48, 125-32, 139-43
Bottles, 84, 147
Bourg, 127
Bourgeais, 42, 48, 127
Bourges, 55
Bourgogne, 120
Bourgogne Aligote, 120
Bourgogne Clairet, 120
Bourgogne Ordinaire, 120
Bourgogne Ordinaire Rosé, 120
Bourgogne Passe-Tous-Grains, 120-21
Bourgogne Rosé, 120

Bourgeuil, 54, 57, 130
Briare, 55
Brinay, 55
Brouilly, 124
Bugey, 137
Burgundy, 28-40, 120-23, 144-46

Cairanne, 133
Cap Corse, 67
Cassis, 26, 37, 79, 134
Cellars, 107-8
Cérons, 46, 125-26
Chablis, 29, 121, 146
Chablis Grand Cru, 121
Chablis Premier Cru, 121
Chambertin, 67, 121
Chambertin-Cos de Bèze, 121
Chambolle-Musigny, 31, 122
Champagne, 60-64, 120
Changurgue, 52
Chapelle-Chambertin, 121
Chardonnay, 33, 63
Charlemagne, 122
Charmes-Chambertin, 121
Chartre, La, 56
Chartreuse, 78
Chassagne-Montrachet, 122
Château de Brissac, 59
Château-Chalon, 52, 65, 137
Château-Climens, 46
Château-d'Yquem, 46
Château-Grillet, 36, 37, 133
Château-Haut-Bailly, 45
Château-Haut-Brion, 44
Chateaumeillant, 55
Châteauneuf-du-Pape, 37, 40, 133
Château-Pape-Clement, 44-45
Château-Rieussec, 46
Châtre, La, 53-55
Chavignol, 55
Cheilly-les-Maranges, 122
Chénas, 35, 124
Chenin Blanc, 59
Chevalier-Montrachet, 122
Chinon, 57, 130
Chiroubles, 35, 124
Chorey-les-Beaune, 122
Chusclan, 133
Clairette de Bellegrade, 134
Clairette de Die, 40, 134
Clairette du Languedoc, 135
Clos de la Roche, 121
Clos de Tart, 121
Clos de Vougeot, 121
Clos des Jasnières, 56
Clos Saint-Denis, 121
Clos-Vougeot, 31
Coggoloin, 32
Cognac, 74-76
Cointreau, 79
Comblanchien, 31
Composition of wine, 113-14
Comté de Nantes, 60
Condrieu, 36, 37, 133
Cooperage, 118
Corks, 83-84
Cornas, 36, 37, 133
Corsica, 67
Corton, 122
Corton-Charlemagne, 32, 122
Coteaux de la Dème, 56
Coteaux de la Loire, 59, 131
Coteaux de la Sarthe, 60
Coteaux de l'Aubance, 59, 131
Coteaux de Touraine, 54, 58
Coteaux du Layon, 59, 131
Coteaux du Loir, 60, 132
Côte-Blonde, 36
Côte-Brune, 36
Côte Chalonnaise, 122-23
Côte de Beaune, 121, 122
Côte de Brouilly, 124

Côte de Nuits, 31, 121
Côte d'Or, 120, 121
Côte du Jura, 136-37
Côte du Thouet, 58
Côte-Rôtie, 35-36, 37, 133
Côte Vermeille, 27
Côtes-Canon, 48
Côtes d'Agly, 25, 28
Côtes de Blaye, 48, 128
Côtes de Bordeaux-Saint-Macaire 126-27
Côtes de Bourg, 127
Côtes de Canon-Fronsac, 128
Côtes de Duras, 49, 50, 136
Côtes de Fronsac, 48, 128
Côtes de Montravel, 136
Côtes du Haut-Roussillon, 25, 28
Côtes du Jura, 65
Côtes-du-Rhône, 35, 37, 133-34
Crème de Menthe, 80
Crepy, 137
Creuzier-le-Vieux, 53
Criots-Bâtard-Montrachet, 122
Crozes-Hermitage, 36, 37, 133
Curaçaos, 79

Decize-les-Maranges, 122

Eaux-de-vie, 73-80
Echézeaux, 121
Entre-deux-mers, 42, 46-47, 126-27
Epernay, 62
Étoile, 137

Fitou, 135
Fixin, 30, 122
Fleurie, 124
Food, 91-97, 100-104
Fronsac, 48, 128
Frontignan, 25, 27

Gaillac, 49, 135
Gard, 40
Gatinais, 55
Gentiane, 79
Gevrey-Chambertin, 31, 122
Gien, 55
Gigondas, 133
Gironde, 125, 139-43
Givry, 123
Glasses, 86-87
Grand Crus, 121
Grand Marnier, 79
Grand Ruoussillon, 25, 135
Grands Echézeaux, 121
Graves, 42, 44-45, 125, 139-41
Graves-de-Vayres, 47, 127
Griottes-Chambertin, 121

Haute-Marne, 120
Haut-Médoc, 43, 125
Haut-Montravel, 136
Hermitage, 37, 133

Jasnières, 54, 132
Juliénas, 35, 124
Jura, 64-66, 136
Jurançon, 49, 51, 136
Jussy, 66

Kirsch, 79

Ladoix, 122
Lalande-de-Pomerol, 129
Languedoc, 26, 134-35
Latricières-Chambertin, 121
Laudun, 133
Ledenon, 40
Lelande-de-Pomerol, 48
Limoux Nature, 135
Liqueur d'Or, 79
Liqueurs, 78-80
Lirac, 134

Loire, 52-60, 129-32
Loiret, 55-56
Loir-et-Cher, 56
Lorraine, 66
Loupiac, 46, 126
Lussac-Saint-Émilion, 129
Lussault, 57

Mâconnais, 33-34, 123
Madiran, 136
Maine, 132
Mandarine, 79
Marc, 77
Marçon, 56
Marsannay-la-Côte, 30
Maury, 25, 27
Mazis-Chambertin, 121
Meac, 48
Médoc, 42, 43-44, 125, 139-41
Menetou-Salon, 130
Mercurey, 122
Meursault, 122
Midi, 24
Monbazillac, 49, 50
Montagne-Saint-Émilion, 129
Montagny, 123
Montbazillac, 136
Monthélie, 33, 122
Montlouis, 54, 57, 130
Montoire, 56
Montrachet, 33, 122
Montravel, 49, 136
Morey-Saint-Denis, 122
Morgon, 124
Moulin-à-Vent, 35, 124
Moulis, 125
Moulis-en-Médoc, 43
Muscadet, 54, 132
Muscadet de Coteaux de Savre et Maine, 60
Muscadet des Coteaux de la Loire, 60
Muscat de Beaumes-de-Venise, 134
Muscat de Frontignan, 27, 134
Muscat de Lunel, 134
Muscat de Saint-Jean-de-Minervois, 135
Musigny, 121

Nantes, 60
Naveil, 56
Neac, 129
Nièvre, 53
Nivernais, 129-30
Nuits-Saint-Georges, 31, 122

Orléans, 55

Pacherenc du Vic-Bilh, 136
Palette, 134
Parfait Amour, 80
Parsac-Saint-Émilion, 129
Patrimonio, 67
Pauillac, 125
Pécharmant, 136
Perigord, 136
Pernard-Vergelesses, 122
Pessac, 44-45
Petit Chablis, 121
Pinard, 70
Pineau des Charentes, 132
Pinot Blanc, 33
Pinot-Noir, 63
Podensac, 46
Pomerol, 129
Pommard, 122
Pouilly-Fuissé, 34, 123
Pouilly-Fumé, 53, 54, 129
Pouilly-Loché, 123
Pouilly-sur-Loire, 53, 129
Pouilly-Vinzelles, 123
Premières Côtes de Blaye, 127

Premières Côtes de Bordeaux, 127
Provence, 40, 134
Prunelle, 79
Puis-seguin-Saint-Émilion, 129
Puligny-Montrachet, 122

Quart de Chaume, 59, 132
Quercy, 136
Quetsch, 79
Quincy, 54, 55, 130

Rasteau, 134
Reuilly, 54, 55, 130
Rheims, 63
Rhône, 35-40, 120, 133-34
Richebourg, 121
Rivesaltes, 25, 28
Romanée-Conti, 121
Romanée-Saint-Vivant, 121
Rosé d'Anjou, 131
Rosé des Riceys, 121
Rosette, 136
Roussilon, 135
Ruchottes-Chambertin, 121
Rully, 123

Sables-Saint-Émilion, 129
Saint-Amour, 124
Saint-Aubin, 122
Sainte-Croix-du-Mont, 126
Saint-Émilion, 42, 47-48, 128-29
Saint-Estèphe, 125
Sainte-Foy-Bordeaux, 47, 127
Sainte-Foy-la-Grande, 42, 47
Saint-Georges-Saint-Émilion, 129
Saint-Hilaire-Saint-Florent, 58
Saint-Joseph, 133
Saint-Julien, 125
Saint-Marcel, 53
Saint-Martin-le-Beau, 58
Saint-Nicolas-de-Bourgueil, 54, 57
Saint-Péray, 36, 37, 133
Saint-Pierre-de-Mons, 45
Saint-Romain, 122
Sampigny-les-Maranges, 122
Sancerre, 55
Santenay, 122
Sâone-et-Loire, 120
Saumur, 54, 58, 131
Saumur-Champigny, 131
Sauternes, 41, 45-46, 126, 141-42
Savennières, 132
Savigny, 122
Savoy, 137
Seine-et-Marne, 120
Seyssel, 137
Sologne, 56
Storage, 87-88

Tache, La, 121
Tavel, 37, 40, 133
Ténarèze, 49, 76
Troo, 56
Touraine, 56-58, 130-31
Tournus, 33

Vacqueyras, 133
Vayres, 127
Vendomois, 56
Vic, 66
Vieille Cure, 78
Villiers-sur-Loir, 56
Vin d'Alsace, 137
Vin de Blanquette, 135
Vin Jaune, 65
Volnay, 33, 122
Vosne-Romanée, 31, 122
Vougeot, 122
Vouvray, 54, 57, 130

Yonne, 120, 121